QUEEN ELIZABETH *the*
QUEEN MOTHER

Dorling DK Kindersley

LONDON, NEW YORK, SYDNEY, DELHI,
PARIS, MUNICH, JOHANNESBURG

An Album of Photographs (pages 5 – 20)
Editors Christina Bankes, Sue Leonard
Picture Researchers Lorna Ainger, Anna Lord
Designer Sarah Mulligan

Chronicle of a Remarkable Life (pages 21 – 120)
Editor-in-chief Christopher Dobson
Index and proof-reading Avril King

First published in Great Britain in 1995 (as Chronicle of the Queen Mother) by
Dorling Kindersley Limited, 9 Henrietta Street, London WC2E 8PS

Reprinted with revisions 2000

2 4 6 8 10 9 7 5 3 1

A CIP catalogue record for this book is available from the British Library

ISBN 0 7513 0824 2

Printed in Italy by L.E.G.O.

see our complete
catalogue at
www.dk.com

PHOTOGRAPHIC CREDITS

While every effort has been made to trace the copyright of photographs, there remains a possibility that an unwitting error has been made in these credits. If this is the case, we apologize for the mistake and ask the copyright holder to contact the publisher so that it can be rectified. The positions of the pictures are indicated as follows: t = top, b = bottom, m = middle, l = left, r = right a = above, x = middle left, y = middle right.

All pictures are from Hulton Getty Collection except:
1 Tim Graham. 7 Tim Graham bl, br. 8–9 Camera Press. 9 Tim Graham mr, br. 11 Tim Graham br. 12 Camera Press tl; Tim Graham mr.
13 Camera Press. 14 Tim Graham tl, tr. 15 Tim Graham. 16 Tim Graham tl; Camera Press bl. 17 Tim Graham tr, br. 18 Tim Graham tl.
20 Camera Press. 23 Popperfoto br. 57 Popperfoto bl. 60 Roger Viollet t. 68 Keystone ml. 72 Popperfoto. 81 Magnum br. 89 Topham br.
95 Topham bl, bx, by, br. 104 Mirror Syndication International br, tr. 105 Syndication International tl; Mirror Syndication International br. 106 Mirror Syndication International bl, tr; Syndication International br. 107 Tim Graham bl. 108 Express Newspapers tl;
Mirror Syndication International tr; Hussein/Sipa Press br. 109 Rex/Sipa Press tl; Mirror Syndication International tr, bl, br.
110 Mirror Syndication International tm; Chernault/Sipa Press bm. 111 Express Newspapers t; Gastaub/Sipa Press br.
112 Rex Features Ltd l, tr, br. 113 Rex Features Ltd m, bl, br. 114 Rex Features Ltd b, tx; Frank Spooner tl, ty. 115 Rex Features Ltd.
Front Cover Tim Graham bl. **Back Cover** Camera Press bl; PA News br.

QUEEN ELIZABETH *the*

QUEEN MOTHER

A Dorling Kindersley Book

Foreword

The lives of certain people mark an era. So it is with Queen Elizabeth, the Queen Mother. The very presence of the "Queen Mum" gives a continuity to life in Britain. She seems to embody all those virtues that the nation holds dear. What makes this all the more remarkable is that when, reluctantly, she came to the throne as consort to King George VI, in 1937, the monarchy was in grave danger. The abdication of Edward VIII had weakened not only the royal family but the whole concept of royalty and there were many who felt that the shy, stammering, new king was not man enough for the job.

It was his wife, mocked by the Duchess of Windsor as "Cookie", who inspired him to set loose the courage hidden by his shyness. Their tour of the United States and Canada immediately before the war was a tremendous political success and their behaviour during the war set an example to the free world. Nothing could better illustrate the British spirit than her actions on the day Buckingham Palace was bombed for the first time. Picking her way through the rubble, she told a policeman: "I'm almost glad we've been bombed. Now I can look the East End in the face." Such defiance caused Hitler to call her "the most dangerous woman in Europe".

By the end of the war, the royal family had never been so genuinely popular, so secure on the throne. Much of the credit must go to her, for she had a natural sense of public relations, of knowing what the people wanted of her. But, behind the smiling exterior, there was a backbone of steel. Anyone harming her beloved Bertie aroused a cold ferocity which harked back to her Scottish warrior ancestry. It was she who insisted that the Duchess of Windsor should not be "Her Royal Highness" and refused to allow the Windsors to return to England in case they should undermine her husband. It took her a long time to forgive Winston Churchill for his support of Edward during the abdication crisis and, if it had been in her power, he would not have become Prime Minister in 1940. She has always been full of warmth and laughter and fun but nobody takes liberties with her.

It was the period after she had come to terms with her husband's death in 1952 that led to her establishment as mother to the nation, not in the imperial sense of Queen Victoria, but in a well-loved, one-of-us sense. She became the "Queen Mum". The people enjoyed seeing her urge her horses home, meeting the Beatles, and greeting well-wishers outside Clarence House on her birthdays. They worried about her illnesses and they felt sorry for her when her family's marriages fell apart in the cruel glare of paparazzi publicity. The camera has been kind to her throughout her life and her magical relationship with her admirers has grown even warmer as each year passes. There is something both nostalgic and comforting about having her around, a reminder of more united times when the nation stood together in the face of danger.

Now, full of years, she is in the golden twilight of a glorious life, one of the last survivors of a remarkable epoch, a century on which she has left a mark as deep as any statesman. "Queen Mum" she may be, but she is also, in Winston Churchill's words, "that most valiant woman".

the QUEEN MOTHER

AN ALBUM OF PHOTOGRAPHS

THE PRIVATE FACE

In the grounds of her London home at 145 Piccadilly, July 1936.

Having fun with Prince Charles at the Little Welsh House, The Royal Lodge, Windsor, April 1954.

With Prince Charles and Princess Anne, watching a meet of the West Norfolk Hunt, January 1958.

A walk with conductor Raymond Leppard (right) on a Norfolk beach, July 1982.

Sheltering from the rain, August 1992.

THROUGH THE GENERATIONS

Top: With Princesses Elizabeth and Margaret at Windsor, 1941.
Above: Striking a dramatic pose for photographer Norman Parkinson 39 years later.

8

An 85th birthday portrait with her grandchildren, photographed by Norman Parkinson, 4 August 1985.

Prince Charles' third birthday, 14 November 1951.

Supported by Prince Charles at the VE Day Thanksgiving service, May 1995.

With Princess Diana and Prince William at the Trooping of the Colour, June 1987.

At a tea party for ex-servicemen in London, December 1932.

Chatting with a land-girl on a mechanical straw baler, harvest time, 1943.

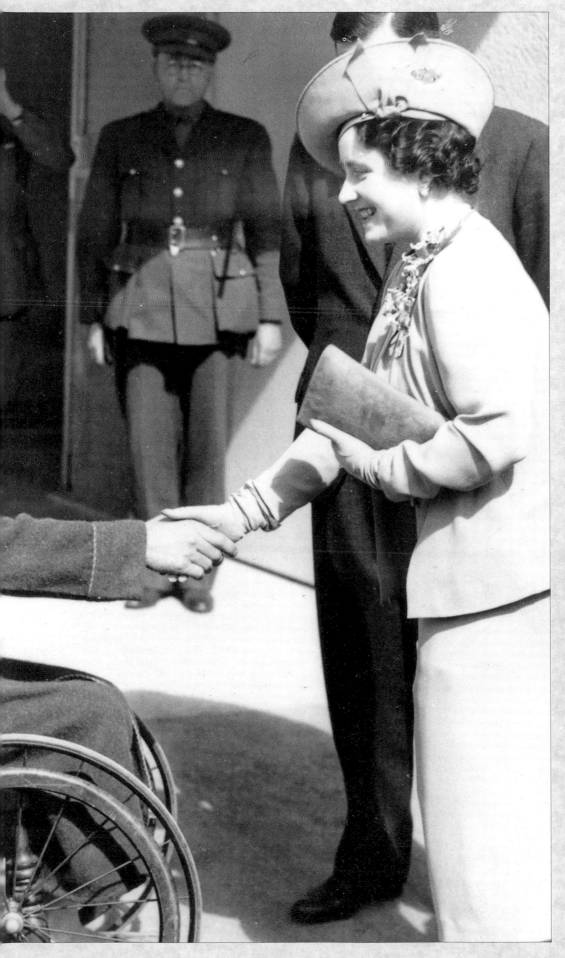

Visiting a wartime emergency hospital, June 1940.

"A gift of H.M. the Queen" — a food convoy on its way to the blitzed East End, March 1941.

An emotional moment at the opening of the VE Day 50th Anniversary celebrations held in Hyde Park, London, 6 May 1995.

FAMILY CELEBRATIONS

With "Bertie" on
their wedding day,
26 April 1923.

Watching over the baby
Princess Elizabeth, 1926.

Celebrating her 92nd birthday at
Clarence House, 4 August 1992.

Mother of the bride when Princess Margaret married Anthony Armstrong-Jones, 6 May 1960.

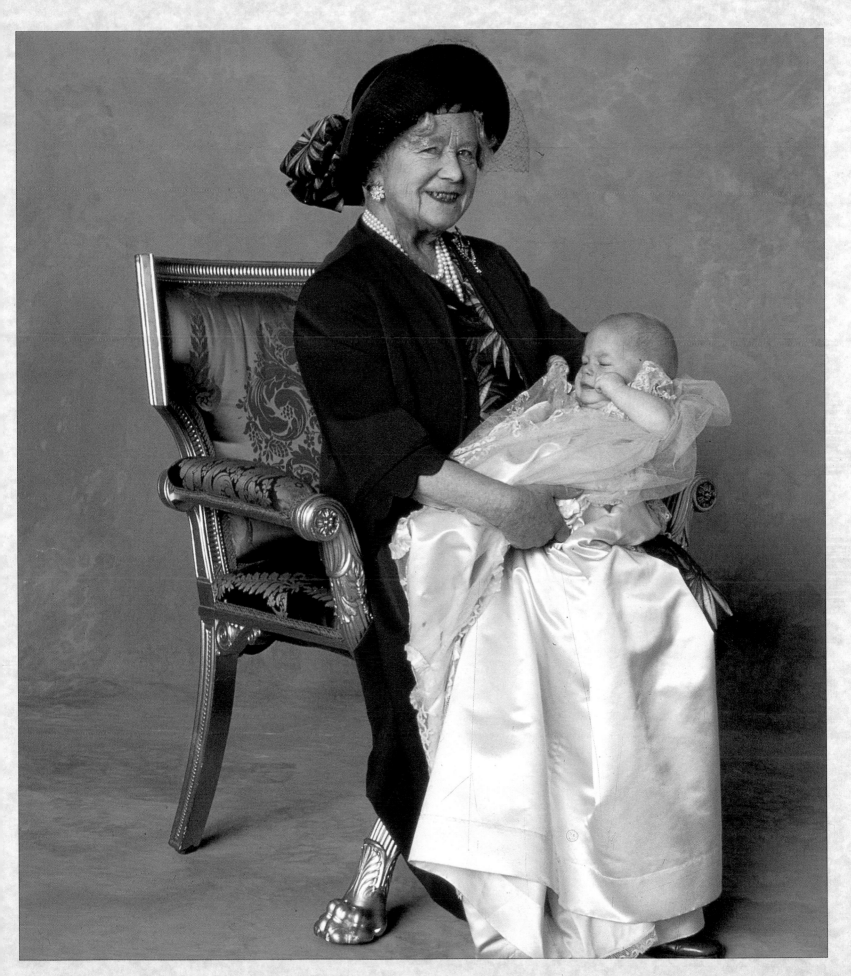

A proud great-grandmother on Prince Harry's christening day, 21 December 1984.

MEETING THE PEOPLE

Impressing the younger generation at a youth club, March 1980.

Young subjects bearing gifts on Sark, May 1984.

A nightmare shared — sympathising with victims of air-raid damage in South London, September 1940.

Showing her love of children at a military hospital in West Germany, March 1984.

COUNTRY LIFE

At the Epsom Derby, June 1985.

With one of her beloved corgis, August 1980.

A good-luck pat for her horse Devon Lock at Sandown Park, January 1956.

In the limelight at Cheltenham, 12 March 1985.

Relaxing away from the crowds at Sandringham.

SERVING THE NATION

Inspecting the Royal Anglican Regiment in Colchester, July 1990.

Down the Great Roan Antelope copper mine in Northern Rhodesia, July 1957.

As Chancellor of the University of London, presenting degrees in May 1956.

*Meeting a group of Maori girls after they had performed
a traditional dance, New Zealand, May 1966.*

The QUEEN MOTHER

Chronicle of a REMARKABLE LIFE

Left: A regal Norman Parkinson birthday portrait, August 1985.

23 Sept 1900. Fifth Congress of the Socialist International meets in Paris.

22 Jan 1901. Queen Victoria dies and a remarkable era comes to an end. She was 81.

9 August 1902. Edward VII, age 60, is crowned at Westminster Abbey. The coronation is delayed because he has to undergo an emergency operation for appendicitis.

17 Dec 1903. Wilbur and Orville Wright fly the world's first heavier-than-air powered aircraft at Kitty Hawk, North Carolina.

8 April 1904. King Edward brings about the *entente cordiale* with France.

28 May 1905. The Japanese navy annihilates the Russian Baltic Fleet at the battle of Tsushima.

19 April 1906. San Francisco is devastated by an earthquake – 1,000 die.

25 July 1907. Sir Robert Baden-Powell, hero of Mafeking, founds the Boy Scout movement.

12 Sept 1908. Winston Churchill marries Clementine Hozier.

25 July 1909. Louis Bleriot crosses the Channel in his flying machine.

6 May 1910. King Edward VII dies and is succeeded by George V.

14 Dec 1911. Norwegian explorer Roald Amundsen beats Captain Scott to the South Pole.

15 April 1912. The "unsinkable" *Titanic* hits an iceberg on its maiden voyage and is lost with more than 1,500 passengers and crew.

4 June 1913. Suffragette Emily Davison is killed when she throws herself under King George's horse during the Derby.

4 August 1914. Britain declares war on Germany.

24 April 1916. Irish nationalists stage uprising in Dublin.

16 March 1917. Tsar Nicholas abdicates.

6 April 1917. US enters war "to save democracy".

3 Jan 1919. Professor Ernest Rutherford splits the atom.

16 Jan 1920. The US introduces Prohibition.

17 March 1921. First birth control clinic opens in London.

A new baby for the new century

Glamis Castle: the historical home of the Bowes Lyons where the young Lady Elizabeth is to spend her childhood.

London, 4 August 1900

A fine daughter was born today to Lord and Lady Glamis in their London home. She is their ninth child and fourth daughter and is to be called Lady Elizabeth Marguerite Bowes Lyon. Her father is heir to the ancient title of the Earl of Strathmore and Kinghorne, and owns rich estates in England and Scotland. They are a family of proud Scottish chieftains and own allegiance only to God and the King. Their main home is Glamis Castle near Dundee, built on the site of a royal hunting lodge. It is a place of ghosts, has a famous monster and is supposedly the scene of the murder of King Duncan by Macbeth, the Thane of Glamis, in 1040.

This late, new baby has emerged into a fresh century and a world of change. Queen Victoria, for so long the symbol of Britain's greatness, is fading away, wearied by her long reign. Germany and the United States are flexing their muscles while the British army seems unable to finish off the Boers despite relieving Ladysmith and Mafeking. Science and technology are the watchwords of this new era. Count Zeppelin has launched an airship and scientists probe the atom. Society is changing too. Oscar Wilde is dying in Paris. Lily Langtry, mistress of the Prince of Wales, has scored a great success in Washington. The cakewalk is all the rage on the dance floor and Britons are sampling a new drink from America, Coca-Cola. In London it is so hot the horses are wearing hats.

1900: The British Army faces a tough enemy in the Boers.

Disgraced, Oscar Wilde is living in penniless exile in Paris.

Lily Langtry, theatrical star and mistress of the Prince of Wales.

Queen Victoria, ruler of the British Empire, dies

Queen Victoria with a bevy of her great-grandchildren at her Osborne home.

The crowned heads of Europe walk behind the coffin of Queen Victoria.

London, 2 February 1901
The crowned heads of Europe followed Queen Victoria's cortege through London today on her last journey from the Isle of Wight to Windsor where she will be buried alongside her beloved Albert. When this tiny woman – "the grandmother of Europe" who, for nearly 64 years, ruled one of the greatest empires the world has ever seen – came to the throne she travelled her realm by coach on rutted roads. She leaves it in the age of the train, the telephone and the motor car. Her successor, Edward VII, who has waited so long to ascend the throne, is a thoroughly modern man. Some think he is too modern with his fast living, his trips to Paris, and his succession of mistresses; others think he has the qualities to lead the Empire "on which the sun never sets" into the new era. He is, for example, fully aware of the military threat posed by his arrogant cousin, Kaiser Wilhelm of Germany, and is determined to make an alliance with France.

King Edward VII succeeds his mother as the ruler of the Empire on which 'the sun never sets'.

The Earl and Countess of Strathmore surrounded by their family at St Paul's Walden Bury where Lady Elizabeth is growing up. She is standing at the knee of her mother who is holding the family's latest addition, David.

Lady Elizabeth enjoys an idyllic Scottish childhood

Little Elizabeth faces the camera.

At an early age, Lady Elizabeth displays her saucy hat sense.

Elizabeth and David in fancy dress.

Glamis Castle, 4 August 1910
Lady Elizabeth Bowes Lyon is 10 today. She has grown into a laughing girl with a mass of dark hair and stunning violet eyes. She spends her time with her younger brother, David, and her mother calls these late-borns her "two Benjamins". They are inseparable, either in the town-house in St James' Square, the Queen Anne house at St Paul's Walden Bury in Hertfordshire, or here, in the Scottish fastness of Glamis which their father inherited when he became the 14th Earl of Strathmore six years ago.

At St Paul's they are schooled by their mother, a French governess and a dancing master and they play in the soft English countryside, but up here, in the hills and heather, they run free, learn to fish for trout and salmon and follow in the pony carts to lay out the lunch when their elder brothers go shooting. Lady Elizabeth is also showing an aptitude for music, loves dressing up for amateur theatricals and has become an expert dancer of Scottish reels.

Her mother, Cecilia, helped by nanny Clara "Alah" Knight, guides all these activities. Of formidable appearance but loving and sensitive nature, the Countess has a simple approach to life: "Life is for living and working at. If you find anything or anybody boring, the fault lies not in them but in you." Lady Elizabeth has less contact with her father, a quiet, conscientious man with an enormous walrus moustache who devotes his time to his estate and to his duties as Lord Lieutenant of Angus. Religion is an unobtrusive part of daily life in the Strathmore household. As far as her father, the Earl, is concerned they live by the traditional family motto: "In thou, my God, I place my trust without change to the end."

In Scotland the young Elizabeth learns country ways from the children of the estate workers, but in London she moves in more exalted circles, attending decorous tea parties in grand houses. At one of these parties given by the Countess of Leicester five years ago she met Prince Albert, the 10-year-old second son of the Prince of Wales. The self-confident young lady, wearing a blue and white dress with a large floppy bow in her hair, took pity on the shy, stammering "Bertie" in his sailor's suit and gave him the crystallized cherries off her sugar cake. It was an act of kindness he has not forgotten.

Romantic young lady growing up.

Raising money for wartime charity.

Blossoming into a real beauty.

A young lady in balldress and pearls.

A young prince in terror of his father

Albert, the sensitive sailor prince.

Buckingham Palace, 4 August 1910
Prince Albert is having a rough time at Osborne, the Royal Naval College. Shy, sensitive and with an appalling stutter, he is bullied by his class-mates even though he is the king's son. Most of his problem stems from the martinet behaviour of his sailor-father who runs his family with an iron hand. He beats his sons and, to cure a congenital defect, forced the prince to wear splints on his legs. Queen Mary is far more affectionate but she dares not cross the king. He loves his sons but domineers them. He once told Lord Derby: "My father was frightened of his mother, I was frightened of my father, and I am damned well going to see to it that my children are frightened of me." He has succeeded. "Bertie" adores him but is terrified of him. Their only bond is the prince's skill with the shotgun.

Prince of Wales, groomed for the throne

Edward, eldest son of King George V.

Dartmouth, 4 August 1910
Prince Edward, the 16-year-old heir to the throne, is completing his naval cadetship with a casual ease. Always called "David" in the royal family, he has a touch of the family shyness but speaks fluently and coherently and his charm is already becoming legendary. He has not, however, totally escaped the effects of his father's strict regime. Courtiers charged with grooming him in kingship note a rebellious streak, a wilfullness which may cause him difficulties when he has to take up the constraints and duties of being ruler of the British Empire. Nevertheless he far outshines his younger brother "Bertie" in everything except sport. Prince Albert may stammer and fail his examinations but he is athletic, moves well, has a good eye for a ball and is determined to win while David is casual.

A crown and ermine robes for the Prince

Caernarfon Castle, 13 July 1911
The 17-year-old Prince Edward, wearing a crown of Welsh gold and dressed in ermine robes, was presented to the Welsh people by his father, King George V, today as Prince of Wales. Showing none of the nervousness that plagues his younger brother, Bertie, he shouted: "Diolch fy nghalon i Hen wlad nhad-ua" [Thanks from the bottom of my heart to the old land of my fathers]. However, what seemed like a traditional ceremony was in fact concoct-ed for the occasion and the Welsh phrase was taught him by that wily politician, David Lloyd George. The young prince was none too pleased by all the fuss, protesting: "What will my navy friends say if they see me in this preposterous rig?" But his protests were to no avail; now that his father is king he has to recognise the dire responsibilities of being heir to the throne. There are advantages; he now has access to the revenues of the Duchy of Cornwall worth some £90,000 a year.

The Tsar loses his crown and is murdered

London, 25 July 1918
King George and Queen Mary attended a memorial service today for Tsar Nicholas and his family, murdered by the Bolsheviks in Siberia. There is no doubt the royal family is deeply shocked by the savage deaths of their Russian cousins since the assassination of any member of Queen Victoria's "European family" affects them all. However, there is a touch of guilt amidst the grief, for last year when Lloyd George supported the Russian provisional government's request for Britain to grant the tsar and his family asylum, the king at first agreed to send a cruiser to fetch them to safety in England but then reneged. Afraid of stirring up revolutionary forces at home during a crucial point in the war, he abandoned "dear Nicky" to his fate. The death of the Romanovs is a dreadful warning to other royal houses caught up in the whirlwind of revolution spawned by the war. It seems that no monarch, however benevolent, is safe on his throne.

King George V presents his son to the people of Wales at Caernarfon Castle.

The Tsar and his children take the sunshine in captivity in Siberia.

The war is over and the world rejoices

Armistice is signed in a railway carriage at Compiègne and the shooting stops.

London, 11 November 1918
The dreadful slaughter of the war came to an end at 11 am this morning. No family has remained untouched. The Strathmores lost one son, Fergus, at the Battle of Loos, and another, Michael, was wounded and captured. Glamis was turned into a military hospital and Lady Elizabeth helped to entertain the wounded soldiers, on one occasion saving the castle by her prompt action when it caught fire. The bravery and patience of the wounded men has impressed her deeply. The royal family also went to war. Prince Albert acquitted himself well at the Battle of Jutland while the Prince of Wales, fretting to get into the front line, served on the staff in France.

Elizabeth's new friend is a royal princess

Queen Mary and her daughter Princess Mary in the fashion at Cowes.

Glamis, September 1919
Lady Elizabeth has made friends with Princess Mary, only daughter of the king and queen, through their mutual interest in the Girl Guide movement. The Guides, founded by General Baden-Powell along with the Boy Scouts, is becoming increasingly popular with boys and girls of all classes. Elizabeth likes it because it encourages the outdoor life which she enjoys so much, and Princess Mary depends on it because it gives her a taste of life outside the strict discipline imposed by her father who frowns on fashionable clothes and parties.

Not blessed with good looks, Mary has the family shyness and dreads making public appearances although she is a fearless horsewoman. The Guides movement is a perfect outlet for her; she can mix with other girls of her age in the anonymity of the blue uniform and her father can find nothing to criticise in its emphasis on duty. Neither can he criticise her friendship with Lady Elizabeth for her father is virtually a king in his own domain. So the two young women exchange visits between Balmoral and Glamis and Elizabeth is increasingly being accepted by the royal family.

An intimate affair: the camera falls in love with Lady Elizabeth

Holyrood Palace, 15 July 1920
Lady Elizabeth made her official deep curtsey as a debutante to the king and queen at this royal palace today. She has grown into a stunning young woman, a trifle plump, but with the flashing violet eyes and dark hair of the true gael. She exudes good health, her sunny temperament shines through and it is these qualities the camera catches. She seems to have an inborn affinity for the lens and falls into a natural pose whenever one is pointed at her. Society women are already marking her as a good catch for their sons, for her own qualities as well as the substantial slice of the Bowes Lyon fortune she would bring to a marriage. The sons, many of them looking for a wife after surviving four years of war, are also smitten but she, still tomboyish, is not ready to settle down yet. Watching her dance a highland reel, one would-be mother-in-law remarked that she would leave a trail of broken hearts behind her. She is also not ready to leave her mother, truly heartbroken by the death of Fergus in the war.

Elizabeth makes a charming pre-Raphaelite study of a Highland lassie.

Dressed up in her Easter bonnet.

Bolsheviks aim at Europe takeover

Moscow, 3 March 1919
Vladimir Lenin, the Bolshevik leader, intends to spread communism throughout Europe. He announced today the establishment of the Communist International, or Comintern, whose function will be to provoke revolutions through agents, propaganda and Moscow gold. Its immediate targets will be countries like Germany and Hungary, devastated by the war, but the Bolsheviks are also aiming at the destruction of the British Empire.

The monster's castle holds no fears for Elizabeth

Glamis Castle, Spring 1922

Glamis goes one better than most castles; they have ghosts, Glamis has a monster – the misshapen son of a Master of Glamis who was born in 1821 but was so hideous that he was shut away in one of the castle's remote rooms and it was declared he had died at birth. But he lived to be 100, dying only last year. It is not known how much Elizabeth knows of her unfortunate kinsman but she has no fear of the castle or its blood-soaked history. She feels safe here and has come home to decide what she is going to do with her life.

She is being pursued with uncharacteristic determination by Prince Albert. They met again two years

'The only woman for Bertie'

ago at a dance and Bertie, about to be made Duke of York, fell head over heels in love with her. He attended all the events where she would be and it soon went round London's fashionable young men that she was "hands off". Word leaked out but the papers got it wrong and suggested that she was involved with the Prince of Wales. She was not his type, however, and his affections were elsewhere, with Mrs Freda Dudley Ward.

Last year Bertie followed Elizabeth to Glamis and formally proposed, but she, fearful of living in the goldfish bowl of royal life,

turned him down. He was disconsolate, but determined. Queen Mary invited herself to Glamis last September to inspect Elizabeth and approved while the king growled that he would be "a lucky fellow if she accepts you". She still hesitates but Bertie is relentless in his pursuit; she is the only woman for him, both families approve of the match and she is weakening.

Lady Elizabeth and the Countess of Strathmore stroll in the grounds of Glamis Castle, historic home of their family.

Lady Elizabeth with protection ancient and modern in the Glamis courtyard.

Mother and daughter admire the view at their castle in Scotland's rolling hills. ▷

Mary's bridesmaid

London, 28 February 1922
Lady Elizabeth's involvement with the royal family became even closer today when she was a bridesmaid at Princess Mary's wedding to Henry, Viscount Lascelles, the eldest son of the immensely rich Earl of Harewood. The wedding has given rise to some ribaldry in smart London circles for Princess Mary is 24 while her bridegroom is nearly 40, and it is said that she agreed to marry him only to escape from her parents who treated her more as the family drudge, carrying out boring duties, than as a royal princess. There is some truth in this gossip for she is a plain woman and had been passed over in the marriage market by eligible European princelings. It is, moreover, certainly true that she

Dressed for the Harewood wedding.

has been desperate to escape the gloomy court life of Buckingham Palace where her father ruled her life even to stipulating the length of her sleeves. Her friendship with Elizabeth opened her eyes to the freedom of life outside the court and she wants to taste it. Her marriage is not, however, a loveless affair. She and her husband are genuinely fond of each other and, while neither of them are passionate people, they should get on well enough. The princess's departure from the palace will probably have an unforeseen effect on Elizabeth, for the Duke of York is now the only one of the royal children still living there. His determination to marry can only be reinforced and there is certainly only one woman for him.

1923

27 Jan 1923. The Nazi party, led by Adolf Hitler, holds its first rally in Munich.

2 March 1923. Matrimonial Causes Bill means wives can now divorce husbands for adultery.

9 March 1923. Lenin quits office after massive stroke leaves him paralysed.

29 March 1923. Paris comes to a halt for the funeral procession of the actress Sarah Bernhardt. "Her voice was liquid gold," said one theatre critic. "She spoke verse as the nightingale sings." She was 78.

14 April 1923. Marathon dancing craze sweeps America.

28 April 1923. Wembley Stadium stages its first sporting spectacular with the Cup Final between Bolton Wanders and West Ham United. Occasion almost ends in disaster when huge crowd of nearly 200,000 spills onto the pitch. Situation saved by a policeman on a white horse who shepherds fans off the pitch. Bolton win 2-0.

21 May 1923. Stanley Baldwin succeeds Andrew Bonar Law as prime minister.

20 July 1923. Pancho Villa, the Mexican revolutionary turned rancher, is shot dead.

2 August 1923. US President Warren Harding dies suddenly, at age 57, after touring Alaska.

12 Sept 1923. The Crown takes over Southern Rhodesia from the British South Africa Company.

16 Sept 1923. Earthquake destroys Tokyo and Yokohama leaving 300,000 dead and 2.5 million homeless.

16 Oct 1923. The government plans to spend £50 million on unemployment relief.

12 Nov 1923. Adolf Hitler and General Erich von Ludendorff are arrested in Munich after their farcical beer-hall putsch.

15 Nov 1923. Inflation in Germany means that a loaf of bread costs 200 billion marks and a construction worker is paid three trillion marks a day.

13 Dec 1923. Lord Alfred Douglas is sentenced to six months in prison for libelling Winston Churchill.

28 Dec 1923. Gustave Eiffel, builder of the tower, dies aged 91.

31 Dec 1923. The literary event of the year is the publication of T.S. Eliot's long poem, *The Waste Land*. Severely criticised by traditionalists, it has become a cult among undergraduates.

Prince Albert woos and wins Elizabeth

Albert and Elizabeth after the royal engagement is officially announced.

London, 16 January 1923
Today's Court Circular announced the engagement of the Duke of York to Lady Elizabeth Bowes Lyon. Bertie has won the love of his life. He proposed to her for the third time in the garden of her parents' home of St Paul's Walden Bury three days ago. He had made up his mind that despite his love for her this would be the last time he would ask her to marry him, but this time she said yes. He was overjoyed and immediately sent a prearranged telegram to his parents saying: "All right. Bertie." They are delighted for him. The Prince of Wales, who, unlike his tongue-tied brother, has great success with women, also approves. Chips Channon, the American-born Tory MP and man about town, records: "There is not a man in England today who doesn't envy him. The clubs are in gloom." Only Elizabeth still has doubts. She has become increasingly fond of Bertie but her acceptance of his proposal comes more from a sense of duty than from love. There is no going back now; she is committed to joining the royal family and is the first "commoner" to do so for 300 years. She will find the royal round with its often irksome duties quite different from her present carefree life, but she has accepted it along with her magnificent engagement ring of blue sapphires. The next step is for her parents to call on their prospective in-laws.

The prospective in-laws come to call on King George and Queen Mary.

Queen Mary is delighted with Elizabeth

The Guides show the way with a present

Elizabeth at Balmoral with Albert, his brother George and Queen Mary.

Elizabeth's Scottish troop parades to wish their leader much happiness.

Sandringham, 20 January 1923
The Earl and Countess of Strathmore, together with their daughter, Lady Elizabeth Bowes Lyon, arrived here today to visit their prospective in-laws, King George V and Queen Mary. Courtiers say the visit is a great success with the king, a stickler for protocol, who warmly welcomed the Scottish "commoners". The imperious Queen Mary, so formidable in her tall hats, pearls and regal manner, whole-heartedly approves of her prospective daughter-in-law. Fearful that her easily-hurt son might fall into the clutches of someone unsuitable from the "fast set", she is delighted with his choice and confides in her diary: "Elizabeth is charming, so pretty & engaging and natural. Bertie is supremely happy." Elizabeth has also won over the gruff king who has made it plain that he hates the thought of "flapper" daughters-in-law. He has even forgiven her an indiscretion which could have proved fatal. A journalist had talked his way into the Strathmores' London home and was about to be thrown out by the butler and Lady Strathmore when Elizabeth appeared, saying, according to the reporter: "Mother, leave this gentleman to me." He then wrote a fulsome account of how she sat at a writing desk with letters and telegrams before her, and naively said: "I suppose you have come to congratulate me? How very kind of you." What he really wanted to know was if it was true she had twice turned down the Duke of

York. She replied: "Now look at me. Do you think I am the sort of person Bertie would have to ask twice?" The king, like his grandmother, was "not amused". There will be no more interviews, but she has the king eating out of the palm of her hand. He tells his diary: "She is a pretty and charming girl & Bertie is a very lucky fellow."

Glamis, March 1923
Lady Elizabeth's Girl Guides have given her one of the first of her wedding gifts, a beautifully made and decorated wooden box. She received it, in uniform, at a parade of the guides and told them how much she would treasure it as a reminder of their happy days together. The presents are characteristic of the givers. Disabled soldiers from the Blighty Works have sent tartan travelling rugs woven with the royal monogram and the Needlemakers Company's present is a thousand gold-eyed needles. The royal family have showered her with fabulous jewels befitting her new status and the Prince of Wales has given the couple a powerful motor car.

On royal duty for the first time: Elizabeth is an instant success

Edinburgh, March 1923
The engaged couple, on a short visit to Glamis, have entranced crowds in Edinburgh where Elizabeth carried out her first royal duties, visiting the McVities bakery. They chose a

design for their wedding cake which is to have four tiers and carry the coats of arms of their two families. Later they went to see Scotland play England at rugby. England won and the Duke of York remarked that for

The engaged couple tour factories in Edinburgh's industrial districts.

once in his life he felt unpatriotic, he wanted his fiancee to see her country win. The Scots are, of course, delighted that one of their countrywomen is to marry the second in line to the throne but she won over the crowds for herself as well as for her origins as she walked, completely at ease, through the crowds while the shy but obviously happy duke followed, allowing her to accept the warmth of the Scottish welcome. Previously, she would shop and visit friends in Edinburgh without being noticed, just another "wee lassie". But now everything has changed. She will not be able to go anywhere without being recognised. She will always be on duty. Everything she wears, every gesture she makes, every word she says in public will be noted and analysed. She is now royal and has become public property. It is a role which will make great demands on her good humour, stamina and shrewdness for she will not only have to play her own role but help sustain her husband.

Glittering royal wedding for Albert and Elizabeth

London, 26 April 1923

Over a million cheering, flag-waving people were lining the streets of London today for the wedding of Albert, the Duke of York, to Lady Elizabeth Bowes Lyon. It was a typical April day, grey early on, but clearing for the bride to leave her parents' house in Bruton Street and drive in a state coach to Westminster Abbey in bright sunshine. Her dress of ivory chiffon moire embroidered with silver thread and pearls had sleeves of lace specially woven in Nottingham and a train of Flanders lace was lent to her by Queen Mary. She carried a bouquet made by the Worshipful Company of Gardeners from white roses and heather to symbolise the union of Scotland and England. As she entered the abbey on the arm of her father, she turned aside and placed her bouquet on the tomb of the Unknown Warrior, perhaps thinking of her brother Fergus, killed in the Great War.

This is the first royal marriage to be celebrated in the abbey since the future Richard II married Anne of Bohemia there, 540 years ago. Since then they taken place in the relative privacy of the Chapel Royal

Albert, newly created Duke of York, poses with Elizabeth and their bridesmaids for their wedding album portrait.

'No broadcast for the pubs'

at Windsor. It was hoped that the ceremony could be made even more public but, while it was recorded on film, the church authorities refused a request from the BBC to broadcast the service live because, "people might hear it while sitting in public houses with their hats on."

The abbey was filled with glittering uniforms and bejewelled women. The king wore the uniform of Admiral of the Fleet, the bridegroom wore the new dress uniform of the fledgling Royal Air Force, and his brothers those of their regiments. The king had asked for the ceremony to be kept as simple as possible without any undue expense but the setting, the vestments and the uniforms with the sun striking through the stained glass windows made it a magnificent occasion.

However, other simpler matters were not forgotten. In his address,

the Archbishop of Canterbury, Cosmo Lang, referred to the duke's work among the underprivileged young people: "You, Sir, have already given many proofs of your care for the welfare of our working people. You have made yourself at home in the mines and shipyards and factories. You have brought the boys of the workshop and the public school together in free and frank companionship. You have done much to increase the public sense of the honour and dignity of labour."

The ceremony over, the guests went directly to Buckingham Palace for the wedding breakfast while the newly-weds rode through the cheering crowds in a coach with huge glass windows. The wedding breakfast consisted of "royal" food: Consomme a la Windsor, Supreme de Saumon Reine Mary, Cotelette d'Agneau Prince Albert, Chapons a la Strathmore and Duchess Elizabeth strawberries. The cake which they had chosen in Edinburgh was nine feet high and slices of identical

cake were distributed to poor children in London and other cities throughout the country.

The celebrations, in compliance with the king's wishes, were over within two hours and the young couple drove away in an open landau through a cloud of rose petals. They will start their honeymoon at Polesden Lacey, a house in Surrey belonging to the brewing heiress and socialite, Mrs Ronald Greville, before moving on to Glamis where the great beacon will be lit in their honour. It has been their day and everybody has enjoyed it, but hanging over it has been the question: when will the Prince of Wales marry and produce an heir to the throne? He was best man to his brother today but there is not the remotest sign of his leading anyone to the altar despite his position, good looks and charisma. *The Times* writes of today's events in its leader column: "There is but one wedding to which (the public) look forward with still deeper interest – the wedding which will give a wife to the Heir to the Throne, and, in the course of nature, a future Queen to England and to the British peoples ... " This is not, however, a problem which worries Bertie and Elizabeth today. They look forward to setting up home; the throne is not for them.

The charismatic Prince of Wales. The people ask: when will he marry?

The great day. Lady Elizabeth leaves for the abbey. The bride arrives in a horse-drawn coach. The ceremony is conducted with regal pomp and circumstance. The newly-weds and their parents pose for the marriage portrait. The couple leave Buckingham Palace in a shower of rose petals to start their honeymoon.

On parade: Elizabeth takes up royal duties

The new Duchess of York posing in her diadem for an official portrait.

London, 30 June 1923
The Duchess of York has barely recovered from an unromantic bout of whooping cough contracted on her honeymoon than she finds herself riding the royal merry-go-round which made her so reluctant to marry the duke. His great aunt, Princess Helena, has died and many of the institutions she supported have asked the duchess to take over her responsibilities. Among them are the Young Women's Christian Association and the National Society for the Prevention of Cruelty to Children. Today she makes her first appearance as a member of the royal family when she accompanies the king and queen and her husband to the RAF pageant at Hendon.

The duchess and her mother at the opening of the British Empire Exhibition.

3 Jan 1924. Tutankhamun's stone sarcophagus is discovered at Luxor.

16 Jan 1924. The Pasteur Institute announces it has isolated the rabies bacillus.

21 Jan 1924. Lenin, father of the Russian revolution, dies aged 54. His death leaves a power vacuum in the Soviet Union which seems likely to be filled by the ruthless Stalin.

22 Jan 1924. Ramsay MacDonald becomes the first Labour Prime Minister of Britain.

3 Feb 1924. Former US President Woodrow Wilson dies, aged 63. He left office in 1920, a sick and disappointed man. "I am a broken piece of machinery," he told a friend a few days ago.

12 Feb 1924. George Gershwin's new composition, "Rhapsody in Blue" is a great hit.

25 March 1924. Greek parliament votes to depose the exiled King George II.

17 April 1924. Mussolini's fascists have scored a sweeping victory in the Italian general election.

23 April 1924. King George opens the British Empire Exhibition at Wembley Stadium by sending a telegram to himself all round the world.

19 June 1924. The climbers George Leigh Mallory and Andrew Irvine are lost on Mount Everest. Last seen disappearing into a cloud only 1,000 feet from the summit, they are feared to be dead.

29 June 1924. The Prince of Wales announces he will start looking for a bride.

20 July 1924. The American Council of Catholic Women opens a campaign for modesty in women's dress.

3 August 1924. The Polish-born British author Joseph Conrad dies aged 66.

18 Sept 1924. Mahatma Gandhi starts a fast in despair at riots between Hindus and Moslems.

24 Oct 1924. Foreign Office publishes "Zinoviev letter" urging revolution in Britain. Moscow says it's a hoax.

5 Nov 1924, China. Boy Emperor Pu-Yi is expelled from the Imperial Palace and all Manchu titles abolished.

20 Dec 1924. Hitler emerges from prison planning to publish his political treatise, *Mein Kampf*, written in his cell.

Smiling Elizabeth charms the crowds

Belfast, 21 July 1924
The Duke and Duchess of York unveiled a war memorial at Queen's University today and honorary degrees were conferred on them. The dean of the law faculty made a particular point of praising the duke for his dedication to public service but it was the smiling duchess the crowd wanted to see. She has been on royal duty for over a year now and she has performed brilliantly.

Her love affair with the camera, evident when she was a child, continues. She seems to know by instinct when to look at the camera, giving photographers every chance to take good pictures. Her warmth is evident wherever she goes, always that smile which lights up her face, the few friendly words, the characteristic wave; she makes an excellent royal ambassador. Her husband has come to rely on her and he has begun to come out of his shell under her encouragement. His stammer is getting better as he builds his fragile confidence. He has told people here: "I am very lucky indeed to have her to help me. She knows exactly what to do and say to all the people we meet."

She has made an equally impressive start to her overseas visits. Last October they travelled to Belgrade where they stood as godparents to the son of King Alexander of Serbia. During the ceremony Bertie saved the infant Prince Paul when the ancient Patriarch of the Serbian Orthodox Church dropped him into the font. They stayed on for the marriage celebrations of Prince Paul of Serbia and Princess Olga of Greece. The duke's Balkan relations agree that she acquitted herself well under close scrutiny.

In private, they lead a quiet life, enjoying the countryside and "solid" friends. She is more artistic than her husband, knowledgeable about modern art and literature; both of them enjoy amateur theatricals. The only cloud on their pleasant life is their home, White Lodge in Richmond Park. Chosen for them by the king, it is uncomfortable, cold and damp. The electrical system is dangerous and the antiquated drains are positively unhealthy. The duchess suffers badly from bronchitis and says the house is "impossible".

Charity events, a vital part of royal duty. Making friends with a donkey at the Fresh Air Fund outing. At a carnival in aid of the Save the Children Fund. Trying her luck at the coconut shy. Visiting the child patients at the Dudley Hospital. Inspecting the guard of honour at the Save the Children Fund fun fair.

1925

Speech disaster for the Duke of York

Wembley, 9 May 1925

The Duke of York's stammer betrayed him cruelly here today when he opened the second year of the British Empire Exhibition of which he is president. Realising the importance of the occasion, he had practised for days to get his speech right, but, overawed by the huge hall, the loud-speakers and the bank of microphones, his fragile confidence deserted him and the stammer, which he has tried so hard to control, made his speech almost incoherent. The more he struggled with his words, the more painful it became for the distinguished audience. The duke's embarrassment was spread to millions of people around the world by the wireless.

None suffered more than his wife who not only gives her support but helps him to write his speeches, using words which do not bring on the stammer. Now it seems that all that good work has been destroyed by one disastrous speech. Many officials and politicians who listened to his excruciating battle to get his words out this afternoon have written him off as unfit for the higher reaches of public life. They think his activities should be confined to opening bazaars. This is especially true of the leaders of the great dominions, Australia and Canada.

'Steel behind the stammer'

If any member of the royal family is going to represent the king in their countries, they want it to be the self-confident, fluent Prince of Wales with whom their soldiers struck up an easy-going rapport during the war. The dangers of today's speech were appreciated and the king listened to it anxiously. He thinks it went not too badly, but one member of the family, the Duchess of York, appreciates the full scale of the disaster. She sat there, smiling brightly, while her husband fought his way through his speech. However, unlike so many others, she knows there is steel as well as goodness in his character and she is determined that they are going to beat the curse of the stammer.

Stutter overcomes Bertie at the opening of Empire Exhibition at Wembley.

Queen Mary and King George at play on the Exhibition's toy town railway.

On safari in Africa: the Duke and Duchess on first Empire tour

Kenya, January 1925

The Duke and Duchess of York are enjoying life in the African bush. They have come here partly to help clear up the duchess's bronchitis and partly to give them some experience of the vast and still powerful British Empire. After a rough Mediterranean crossing, the P&O liner *Mulbera* took them via the Suez Canal to Aden, then round the Horn of Africa to Mombasa, where they were welcomed by the Governor of Kenya, Sir Robert Coryndon, and 5,000 dancing Africans. The governor's train took them to Nairobi through an untouched landscape filled with zebra, giraffe, wildebeest and lions with Mount Kilimanjaro looming in the distance.

They are on safari now, sleeping under canvas and riding mules through the bush. The duke, an excellent shot, has had fine sport. His trophies include a rhinoceros which, wounded, charged him and he brought it down only 30 yards away. The duchess has used her camera more than her rifle. They are also carrying out a few official functions,

Elizabeth and Bertie visiting the Makwar dam with colonial officials.

including a visit to the Makwar dam, one of Africa's great engineering achievements. Soon they will leave for Uganda, where the duchess is hoping to try her fishing skills on Lake Albert, and then will travel a thousand miles along the Nile into the Sudan where the desert capital of Khartoum is planning a welcome with fireworks and illuminations. They will then ride the caravan route to the Red Sea to take the ship for home. They are entranced by the land and its people and have gained much insight into the workings of the empire.

Travelling royals, from safari in Africa to shooting in Scotland

Smart young things: The Yorks arrive at Glamis for the 'Glorious Twelfth'.

Glamis, 12 August 1925

The "wee lassie" and her husband have come home to Scotland for the "Glorious Twelfth" after their adventures in Africa. Considered one of the best shots in Britain, the duke is looking forward to the shooting on the Glamis estate where the grouse are abundant and hare offer a good test of marksmanship. There will be some deer-stalking too, nothing as exciting or dangerous as facing a charging rhino but a fine stag is no mean quarry. The duchess will not take part in these activities for she hopes she is pregnant and is content to spend time strolling through the castle's grounds. No announcement will be made, but as soon as her pregnancy becomes obvious she will retire discreetly from public life for it is thought unseemly for pregnant royal women to be seen by the public. It is some consolation to them both that Bertie has recovered his nerve after the Wembley disaster, making three broadcasts without mishap, but he is still struggling to control his stammer and needs professional advice.

Duchess on duty back in England

London, Summer 1925

After the excitement of their visit to Africa, the Yorks have settled into the routine of royal life at home. It is a mixture of quiet domesticity, court ceremonial and an astonishing variety of official duties. They have planted trees, visited factories, attended displays at schools for orphans, opened nurses' homes, presented prizes at agricultural shows, lunched with mayors and dined with foreign rulers. They have shaken a thousand hands, smiled a million smiles, honoured wherever they go but scrutinised by those who honour them. The duchess has survived this ordeal with flying colours. *The Times* says of her: "She lays a foundation stone as though she had just discovered a new and delightful way of spending an afternoon."

King George is pleased with their double-act. Despite the Wembley debacle, he has come to look on his second son as far more reliable than his heir who is becoming capricious in the performance of his duties. He is even more pleased with Elizabeth's performance and she, quite unafraid, has him doting on her. She is notoriously unpunctual while he is obsessed with good time-keeping. Awestruck courtiers tell the story of the time she came down late for dinner; everybody expected an explosion from the king but he waved her apologies aside: "Not at all, my dear. We must have sat down too early."

Presenting Charter to Ilford.

1926

27 Jan 1926. Moving pictures transmitted by wireless are demonstrated at the Royal Institution in London by scientist John Logie Baird. He calls his invention "television".

9 Feb 1926. There is severe flooding in London suburbs after 18 days of continuous rain.

1 March 1926. British government recognises Sheik Ibn Saud as King of the Hejaz, now called Saudi Arabia.

6 March 1926. The Shakespeare Memorial Theatre at Stratford-on-Avon is destroyed by fire.

25 April 1926. Ali Reza Khan, a former cavalryman, has himself crowned Shah of Persia at the Imperial Palace in Teheran.

5 May 1926. First General Strike in British history began at midnight.

25 June 1926. Bobby Jones, a 25-year-old lawyer from Atlanta, Georgia, becomes the first amateur to win the Open, golf's greatest prize.

23 July 1926. Benito Mussolini says Italy must expand or suffocate.

6 August 1926. Gertrude Eberle, 19-year-old New Yorker, becomes the first woman to swim the Channel.

23 August 1926. Actor Rudolph Valentino, the "Latin Lover" dies of a ruptured appendix. He was only 31.

1 Sept 1926. The Prince of Wales and his younger brother, Prince George, come to the end of a month-long visit to Canada celebrating Canada's diamond jubilee during which the prince buys a ranch in Calgary.

1 Oct 1926. Alan Cobham lands his tiny seaplane on the Thames at Westminster to complete a record 28,000 miles round-trip to Australia.

18 Nov 1926. George Bernard Shaw's refusal to accept his Nobel Prize money of £7,000 is causing general embarrassment. The Royal Swedish Academy cannot dispose of the money except to him and he is inundated with begging letters. He says: "I can forgive Alfred Nobel for having invented dynamite, but only a fiend in human form could have invented the Nobel Prize!"

20 Nov 1926. Imperial conference in London decides that Canada, Australia, New Zealand, South Africa and Newfoundland will become self-governing dominions.

Birth brings joy, strike brings fear

The Duke and Duchess of York's first baby is christened Princess Elizabeth.

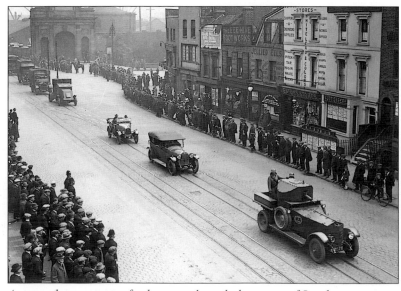

Armoured cars escort a food convoy through the streets of London.

London, 21 April 1926

The Duchess of York gave birth to a daughter in the early hours of this morning at the Bruton Street house of the Strathmores. The birth, by caesarean section, was difficult but the baby is healthy. Queen Mary records that she is "a little darling with a lovely complexion and pretty fair hair". She is to be called Elizabeth Alexandra Mary after her mother, grandmother and great-grandmother and will be third in line to the throne after the Prince of Wales and her father. It is not expected that she will ever come to the throne, however, for it is assumed that the Prince of Wales will soon marry and produce his own children who will take precedence. If the Duke and Duchess of York have a son, he too, would take precedence over his elder sister, so the prospect of England being ruled by another Queen Elizabeth would seem remote.

News of the birth broke too late for it to be carried by the morning papers, but the word spread swiftly and an enthusiastic crowd braved the rain in order to celebrate outside 17 Bruton Street where the Yorks have been living comfortably, having fled the unhygienic horrors of the White Lodge.

Revolution?

Despite the cheers of the crowd, the baby's birth has been overshadowed by the threat of a national coal strike and the prospect of the first General Strike in Britain's history. There is much distress in the country and the authorities are fearful that a strike will lead to class warfare and an attempt by the Bolsheviks to bring revolution to the streets of Britain. Twelve leading communists have already been imprisoned under the Incitement to Mutiny Act. The army is making preparations, tanks and armoured cars are being stationed at strategic points. Plans have been made for an emergency system of transport with volunteer drivers. The mood of the workers is more a desire for justice than revolution but there is fear in Westminster that the crowd cheering the birth of Princess Elizabeth today could soon turn into a mob, baying for blood.

Ceremony for proud mother and daughter

Duchess and Princess Elizabeth leave their London home for the christening.

London, 29 May 1926
Princess Elizabeth Alexandra Mary, wearing the cream satin and Honiton lace robe first worn by Queen Victoria's children, was christened today in the private chapel inside Buckingham Palace. The ceremony was carried out by the Archbishop of Canterbury with purified water from the River Jordan in a gold, lily-shaped font brought from Windsor Castle for the occasion. Her godparents could hardly have been grander: King George and Queen Mary, Princess Mary, the Duke of Connaught, Elizabeth's sister, Lady Elphinstone, and the Countess of Strathmore. The baby cried so lustily throughout the ceremony that her nurse dosed her with the old-fashioned country remedy of dill-water. It had no effect.

The Duke of York had written to his father for his approval of her names: "I hope you will approve of these names & I am sure there will be no muddle over the two Elizabeths in the family. We are so anxious for her first name to be Elizabeth as it is such a nice name & there has been no one of that name in your family for such a long time. Elizabeth of York sounds so nice too." The king was happy to agree. He was also happy to see the crowd of well-wishers outside the palace. The strikers, with whom he has much sympathy, have gone back to work without any violence. Only the miners remain out.

A cuddly present for the new baby.

Bertie takes sporting humiliation to heart

Wimbledon, 30 June 1926
The Duke of York's passion for tennis undid him here today when he and his partner, Louis Greig, were trounced 6-1, 6-3, 6-2 in the first round of the men's doubles by the veterans A.W. Gore and H. Roper Barrett who, at 58 and 52, are over 20 years older than their opponents. The duke and Greig are competent players, having won the RAF doubles six years ago, but it was unfortunate for them that they came up against Gore, a three-times winner of the men's singles, and Roper Barrett, who had won the doubles three times. In this, the jubilee year of the All England Lawn Tennis Club, the organisers were delighted with the royal entry and wanted to put the match on the Centre Court. The duke wanted an outside court, so they compromised with No 2 Court. Alas, the duke and his partner were outclassed before an increasingly restive crowd. At one point, when the left-handed duke had mishit several shots, a wag in the stand shouted: "Try the other hand, Sir." He takes his tennis seriously, often playing before breakfast and inviting professionals to play on

Thrashed at Wimbledon tournament.

the courts at Buckingham Palace. Consequently, his one-sided defeat today has sparked off one of his fits of rage known to the royal family as his "gnashes". He has vowed never to play in public again and Louis Greig, who, as comptroller of his household, has served him loyally as servant and friend, has fallen out of favour.

Getting her hands dirty on the footplate

Ashford, Kent, October 1926
The Duchess of York has resumed her round of royal duties following the birth of her daughter. Among them was her initiation, for which she was suitably robed, into the poetic mysteries of the Welsh National Eisteddfodd in Swansea. Another was to ride on the footplate of the *Lord Nelson* at Southern Railway's locomotive works. She coped with both with equal good humour.

The Duchess on the 'Lord Nelson', the most powerful engine in the country.

Albert and Elizabeth sail to represent

Crossing-the-line fun on the high seas

The Equator, 2 February 1927
HMS *Renown*, carrying the Duke and Duchess of York on their State visit to New Zealand and Australia, reached the equator today and, according to naval custom, the royal couple underwent the ceremony of crossing the line. The duke, suitably dressed, was lathered with a distemper brush, shaved with a huge wooden razor by "King Neptune" and his followers and then ducked. He is now an "Old Sea Dog". The duchess was treated more gently, touched with sea water, and awarded the Order of the Golden Mermaid.

A drink for the Duchess ...

... and a shave for the Duke.

From one chief to another, a symbol of homage and affection

Suva, February 1927
In a day devoted to the expression of the friendship between the two kingdoms of Fiji and Great Britain, Ratu Popi Seniloli, grandson of King Cakadau, presented the Duke of York with a "tabus", a sperm whale's tooth, the traditional symbol of homage and affection. The duke made a neat little speech of thanks on behalf of his father and, at ease in the friendly atmosphere, his stammer was hardly noticeable. He then "drank himself in" as paramount chief with a bowl of kava, the potent local liquor. This was the signal for the start of a tremendous kava party in which everybody joined and British official protocol disappeared in the foot-stamping dancing of the Fijians. Tonight, the royal couple were escorted back to *Renown* by torch-bearers and warriors chanting songs of farewell.

The Duke of York receives a 'tabus', the tooth of a sperm whale, during a stop-over at Suva in the Fiji Islands.

King George in the Land of the Long White Cloud

Fijians fall for Duchess' violet eyes

HMS *Renown*, February 1927

The duchess was a great success at Suva, the warmth of her smile and her celtic violet eyes causing much favourable comment. It was agreed that she is a fitting bride for a chief. She was given a number of presents, among them a red coral crown and and a model canoe which was pulled across the lawn of Government House by two lines of Fijian women. The canoe has now been set up on the deck of *Renown* on a sea of waves made from sailcloth, with the duchess, impeccably dressed for afternoon tea, sailing her own canoe.

A picture for the sailors: Elizabeth sails her Fijian canoe on a mock sea.

The big fish that didn't get away

Lake Taupo, February 1927

The Duchess of York, looking distinctly unroyal in her old macintosh, has been fishing for the huge rainbow trout that live in this lake on New Zealand's North Island. Guided by a local expert, she landed a beauty after an exciting fight. Her brothers taught her to fish in the cold rivers round Glamis and she is expert at fly-fishing for trout and salmon. Given the choice between a smart Mayfair cocktail party and a day on the river in her oldest clothes, hat pulled down over her ears, she will choose the river every time. She loses herself there, concentrating on the fly and the fish, nothing else matters. She has not, however, experienced anything like fishing for the Lake Taupo trout before. They are special. A two-pounder in Scotland is a good fish; here the trout are the size of salmon and catching them becomes an obsession. "She'll be back," said a local, knowingly.

Duke and Duchess get a tumultuous welcome in New Zealand

Invercargill, 21 March 1927

The visit of the Duke and Duchess of York to New Zealand has been a tremendous success. Given a tumultuous reception when they arrived at Auckland on 22 February, they have not put a foot wrong. The duke, sometimes making three speeches a day, is delighted with his performance. He owes much to Australian speech therapist Lionel Logue who, called in by the duchess after the Wembley debacle, has been treating the duke in London. Only once has the duke's confidence failed him and that was when his wife fell ill with tonsillitis and had to cancel all her engagements. The duke, certain that the crowds turned out only to see her, and fearful that he could not carry on without her, wanted to cancel the tour. She insisted that he continue and, in the event, her absence proved to the astonished duke that he could go it alone despite shouts from the crowds of: "We want the duchess."

Their first series of engagements were in Rotorua where they visited the volcanic hot springs and a Maori settlement where the warriors performed the *Haka* war dance for them, and the duke thanked them in Maori. They moved on to sheep country where "Canterbury Lamb" comes from and the duke had a splendid trip to Christchurch, taking the place of the engine-driver on the royal train to drive it through the longest tunnel in the empire. He emerged from the tunnel, smoke-stained and grimy but grinning with schoolboy happiness.

The duchess is delighted that Bertie is doing so well, but there is a certain sadness behind her smile: she misses her daughter terribly. She was so affected when she kissed six-month-old Elizabeth goodbye that she had to be driven several times round Grosvenor Square to compose herself before facing the official farewells. The New Zealanders have not helped her to forget. The crowds shout: "Three cheers for the baby at home." And wherever she goes she is given dolls for her daughter.

King George is keeping a close eye on their progress and, although he has the annoying habit of watching the newsreels to pick on tiny faults in dress and ceremonial protocol, he is well pleased with the courageous way in which his son is sticking to his task. He should be. The duke and duchess have done a splendid job here, summed up by a huge banner displayed at one town: "Tell the King we're loyal".

Smiling Elizabeth inspects overawed pack of Wolf Cubs in Wellington.

Elizabeth lands a fine trout.

Despite their fears, Aussies fall for royal couple

Bertie and Elizabeth wave to the crowd at Maitland, New South Wales.

Canberra, 9 May 1927

The Duke and Duchess of York have triumphantly brought off the most important engagement of their tour, the opening of Parliament House in this new capital city of Canberra. This was the occasion that the Australian Prime Minister Stanley Bruce feared would end in disaster with the duke tongue-tied in front of thousands of Australians who had really wanted the Prince of Wales to open their new parliament. But the duke, who has grown in stature throughout the tour, made an excellent speech praising the building of Canberra: "a great landmark in the history of Australia". He felt so confident that he made a second, unscheduled, speech to the 20,000 people gathered outside.

The people had poured into the city, camping out to watch the proceedings. They were not disappointed. The duke and duchess drove up in an open carriage. Australia's own Dame Nellie Melba sang the National Anthem and the duke unlocked the new building with a golden key to a great roar from the crowd. It has been like this all the way through their tour. News of their success in New Zealand spread across the Tasman Sea and when *Renown* steamed into Sydney Harbour in

Ready for inspection in Adelaide.

brilliant sunshine, the guns thundered, the bells pealed and at a public reception thousands of people marched four abreast, arms linked, past the reviewing stand.

The Aussies quickly took to Elizabeth who was named "the smiling duchess" by the newspapers. After their visit to South Australia, Sir Tom Bridges, the governor, wrote to King George: "The duchess has had a tremendous ovation and leaves us with the responsibility of having a whole continent in love with her." On ANZAC day, the National Day of Remembrance, the duke took the salute at the Cenotaph in Melbourne where 30,000 ex-servicemen, led by 29 holders of the Victoria Cross, marched past in a moving demonstration of loyalty.

Tomorrow the duchess is to plant two trees, one of them a willow from London's Kew Gardens, in what will become Canberra's central park. The royal couple will then go north to Perth where they will spend an evening with 3,000 ex-servicemen at a variety show before boarding *Renown* for the long voyage home. This tour, which has lasted for six arduous months, has been a brilliant diplomatic success, linking the southern dominions even closer to the mother country. The doubts about the duke's ability have been replaced by appreciation of his courage and hard work. And, as Sir Tom Bridges reported to the king, everyone is in love with "the smiling duchess".

Duke opens the new federal Parliament building in the Australian capital of Canberra and makes a fluent speech.

The journey comes to an end, a welcome awaits

They're off! Enjoying a day at the races

Adelaide, 4 May 1927
The royal visitors took a day off from speeches and ceremonial today to watch the Adelaide Cup at the Morphettville Race Course, building yet another bond with the Australians, for there are few things a "fair dinkum" Aussie likes more than a day at the races. And that is also true of the duchess. The Bowes Lyons are a racing family and their colours, blue with buff stripes and a black cap with a gold tassel, are well-known on Britain's courses. The duke, too, has horse-racing in his blood. His grandfather, Edward VII, was one of the most successful owners of his day with his appropriately named Diamond Jubilee winning five major races, including the 2,000 Guineas, the Derby and the St Leger in 1900. That same year his Ambush II won the Grand National steeplechase. Neither the duke nor the duchess own race-horses yet, although she is an expert horse-woman and he is a fearless polo player. For the moment they have enough to do with their increasingly busy round of royal duties and their young daughter. However, judging from the enthusiasm with which the duchess urged home the winner today, joining in the cheers of the enthusiastic racegoers, it would not require much persuasion for her to take up the "sport of kings".

Watching the Adelaide Cup at the Morphettville Race Course.

Home Sweet Home from Down Under

London, 27 June 1927
The duchess has had a joyous reunion with the baby daughter she has not seen for six months. She delighted the welcoming crowd today by bringing Princess Elizabeth out in the rain to join her husband in waving from the balcony of their new London home at 145 Piccadilly. They had an adventurous trip home when a serious fire broke out in the engine-room of HMS *Renown* 1,100 miles from land between Perth and Mauritius. It took 12 hours to put out and the duchess said she knew it was serious because people kept assuring her it was not. For the rest of the voyage, they recovered from the rigours of their travels, playing deck games and taking part in amateur theatricals with the crew of the battleship. There can be no doubt that their visit has been a great success. When they left Perth six weeks ago, thousands of people lined the shore to sing "Auld Lang Syne" and "Will Ye No Come Back Again". When the *Renown* docked at Portsmouth their welcome was more formal but no less significant. The duke's three brothers welcomed them at the quayside and the king and queen were waiting to greet them when their train arrived at Victoria Station. The king has privately expressed his pleasure at the way the duke conducted himself and his affection for his daughter-in-law is plain to see. But now, all she wants to do is be with her daughter.

Playing deck quoits on the journey home on board HMS 'Renown'.

Reunited with her baby, Elizabeth acknowledges crowd's welcome.

Jazz Age comes in with jungle beat

New York, December 1927
Jazz – foot-tapping, syncopated dance music – is the musical phenomenon of the year. Duke Ellington, the black jazz composer, has the whole of New York, black and white, travelling up to Harlem where his 11-piece group is producing his "jungle jazz" at the Cotton Club. His special sound is created by growling brass, tom-toms and "wa-wa" mutes. Downtown, Paul Whiteman and his orchestra are playing what he calls "syncopated jazz" with trumpeter Bix Beiderbecke, trombonist Tommy Dorsey and a group called the Rhythm Boys which includes a young singer called Bing Crosby. In Chicago, Louis Armstrong, a dexterous cornet player with a voice like a barrel of gravel, has a smash hit with "St James's Infirmary Blues".

The Colonel inspects her regiment

London, August 1927
As a mark of his appreciation of the Duchess of York's success on the Australasian tour, King George has made her Colonel-in-Chief of one of his "own" regiments, the King's Own Yorkshire Light Infantry. Elizabeth is delighted for it is a proud regiment with a fine fighting reputation, and many of its men are drawn from an area where her family has historic connections. The duchess is no stranger to military matters; her brothers served in the Black Watch and she learnt about the fortitude of soldiers when Glamis was turned into a military hospital during the war. She is also to take over the presentation of sprigs of shamrock to the Irish Guards on St Patrick's Day, a tradition started by Queen Alexandra in 1901.

With the KOYLIs at Aldershot.

The King melts before Elizabeth's charms

Balmoral, September 1927
Elizabeth has worked her magic on her father-in-law as well as her husband. It is noticeable that when they are together the gruff old king, a tyrant to his own sons and daughter, relaxes and takes pleasure in her presence. Courtiers are amazed at the way she can twist him round her little finger. Much of her success stems from the fact that she is not frightened of him and, while paying him the respect due to a king, is perfectly open and natural in his company. What really impresses him, however, is the speed with which she has learnt the business of being royal and the ease with which she carries out her duties. "People like her," he says, "and she seems to like them, whoever they are." He compares her favourably with the women who form the "Prince of Wales' set" round his eldest son with whom he is becoming more and more disillusioned. The king and his heir seem hardly able to bear each other's company. The cumulative effect of this rift, the high regard in which the king holds Elizabeth, the confidence with which she has imbued her husband, and the love the king has for his grand-daughter "Lilibet" has been to foster a growing appreciation between Bertie and his father where before there was simply duty and familial love. On this holiday in Scotland father and son have discovered that they can talk together as adults and the king is taking pleasure in the company of Bertie – as well as Elizabeth.

Elizabeth and her father-in-law at a charity fete on the grounds of Balmoral.

Nation waits anxiously while doctors fight for the King's life

Newspapers telling the story of King George's serious illness are snapped up.

London, 23 November 1928
The king is dangerously ill. Last night his doctors rushed to his bedside at Buckingham Palace, and the Prince of Wales has been summoned home from his African tour. The king has been suffering from a fever and congestion of the lungs following chronic bronchitis and his condition has deteriorated rapidly in the last two days. One of the new X-ray machines has been set up in the palace to help discover the seat of the infection. Meanwhile the nation waits anxiously for news.

Turning her charm on the ordinary people

Paying a surprise visit to the Queen Alexandra Home for Wounded Soldiers.

Opening the Child Haven at Hutton.

London, Summer 1929
The "smiling duchess" has achieved a quite remarkable popularity with the British people as well as with the king and queen. Always impeccably dressed, always eager to listen, she goes about her ever-increasing duties with a combination of approachability and serenity that no other member of the royal family has been able to achieve. "She's a corker" is the popular judgement. She is helped by the obvious happiness of her marriage and the fairy-tale beauty of Princess Elizabeth who made the cover of *Time* magazine on her third birthday. Crowds call out for "Lilibet" whenever she travels with her parents. The duke has also become popular with the people who appreciate his efforts to break down social barriers with his annual camp in which 200 working class boys under the auspices of the Industrial Welfare Society and 200 boys from public schools go under canvas together. Despite some misgivings from the palace, the duke spends several days with the boys and the project is proving a great success.

Royal connoisseurs admire amateur artists

London, March 1928
Queen Mary and the Duchess of York have given their support to the Civil Service Art Society which is holding an exhibition at the Victoria and Albert Museum. The duchess has brought a love of the arts into a royal family not noted for its intellectual or artistic qualities. Queen Mary certainly has an appreciation of fine things but it is usually of the jewels in her magnificent collection. The duchess is different; she plays the piano well, is knowledgeable about modern art and keeps up with the literary world. She enjoys the company of artists and writers and often surprises them with her knowledge of their work.

At the Civil Service Art Exhibition.

Family affair: her brother David marries

London, February 1929
David Bowes Lyon, the favourite brother of the Duchess of York, has married Rachel Spender-Clay. Her father is a Member of Parliament, a Privy Councillor and a Lt. Colonel and represents precisely the middle-England in which the duchess feels most at home. She has come to rely on David as a shrewd and discreet adviser who can offer opinions from sources outside the royal family's courtiers who sometimes seem to be divorced from the real world. He is also building a career in merchant banking with contacts all round the world who provide an alternative view of international affairs to that of the foreign office. He has no official position but he has begun to play an important role in the York's inner household.

Elizabeth and Bertie leaving St Margaret's, Westminster, after the wedding of David Bowes Lyon.

Inspecting flats for Kensington's housing trust after opening Crosfield House.

Wall Street crashes on Black Thursday

New York, 24 October 1929
In a wave of panic selling, some 13 million shares changed hands on the New York Stock Exchange today sending prices crashing as investors ordered: "Sell at any price." A number of speculators have committed suicide and police riot squads were called in to disperse the hysterical crowds gathering in Wall Street for news of emergency measures being taken by an hurriedly convened meeting of bankers. Prices recovered when Thomas W. Lamont, senior partner of J.P. Morgan, emerged from the meeting with bland assurances. "There has been a little distress selling on the Stock Exchange," he said, adding that the situation was "technical rather than fundamental". Despite his soothing words it is obvious that the era of easy-money and over-confidence is finished and with it goes the dreams of an army of small investors, many of whom have lost everything.

31 Jan 1930. The Five Power Naval Conference meets in London to try to control the arms race which, says King George, "has led to a feeling of insecurity between nations and even to the risk of war".

10 March 1930. Unemployment in the UK has risen to 1.5 million as world economy slumps.

11 April 1930. US scientists predict that man will land on the moon by the year 2050.

24 Sept 1930. The Duke of York takes over from the Prince of Wales as captain of the Royal and Ancient Golf Club.

4 Oct 1930. The R.101, the world's biggest airship, crashes in France on a voyage from England to India; 44 die.

1 May 1931. President Hoover opens the tallest building in the world, the 1,245-foot Empire State Building in New York.

24 August 1931. The Labour government falls and Prime Minister MacDonald forms a National government.

18 Sept 1931. The Duke and Duchess of York visit their new home, The Royal Lodge in Windsor Great Park. It is in a ruinous state but they fall in love with it.

30 Sept 1931. Unemployed stage demonstrations throughout the country and 12,000 naval ratings mutiny at Invergordon in protest at government's austerity programme.

2 March 1932. The 20-month-old son of "Lone Eagle" Charles Lindbergh is kidnapped from the Lindbergh home. Gangster Al Capone offers $10,000 reward for baby's safe recovery.

April 1932. The Duchess of York engages Miss Marion Crawford as governess. She is immediately dubbed "Crawfie".

8 Nov 1932. Franklin Delano Roosevelt becomes President of the United States.

25 Dec 1932. King George V broadcasts Christmas greetings to the nation for the first time.

28 Jan 1933. The Duchess of York meets Mrs Wallis Simpson at Fort Belvedere, the Prince of Wales's house near Windsor.

30 Jan 1933. Adolf Hitler is appointed Chancellor of Germany.

5 Dec 1933. Prohibition ends in the United States.

New baby, new house, new life!

Glamis Castle, 22 August 1930

The Duchess of York gave birth to her second daughter here last night amidst the thunder and lightning of a violent summer storm. It was the special wish of the duchess to have her second baby in this romantic place which holds so many happy memories for her, and the king granted her permission for the royal baby to be born in Scotland. The duchess was a fortnight late in giving birth and so caused some discomfort to two men, J.R. Clynes, the home secretary, and Harry Boyd, the ceremonial secretary at the home office. The law requires that the home secretary be present at a royal birth, a tradition begun after rumours in 1688 that a baby was smuggled into the royal bed chamber in a warming pan. So, on 5 August the two men journeyed north to stay at Airlie Castle some eight miles from Glamis. For 15 days they kicked their heels; then, when the summons came, they had to make a hair-raising high-speed drive through the thunderstorm. They arrived with 20 minutes to spare. Tonight Scotland is celebrating the birth of a royal princess on Scottish soil. The great beacon on Hunter's Hill is to be lit and many drams are being taken in the new baby's honour. She has already caused a problem for her proud parents. They were so certain the baby would be a boy that they had not chosen any girls' names. The duchess then decided she wanted to call her daughter Ann Margaret because: "I think that Ann of York sounds pretty, and Elizabeth and Ann go so well together." But the

The Duchess of York's new child is named Princess Margaret Rose.

king, who usually enjoys humouring his daughter-in-law, does not approve of Ann as a royal name and so she is to be Princess Margaret Rose. With their growing family the Yorks must now find a nanny and, more importantly, find a house on the outskirts of London where they can bring up their daughters while carrying out their royal duties.

'Crawfie' becomes governess.

The Yorks are delighted with their new home, The Royal Lodge, Windsor.

Paris welcomes Albert and Elizabeth

Paris, July 1931

Enthusiastic crowds have welcomed the Duke and Duchess of York to Paris where the royal couple are visiting the Colonial Exhibition, a display of the achievements of the French empire. They are being guided on their visit by the veteran Marshal Lyautey, founder of modern Morocco and one of the most successful colonial administrators of all time. At a dinner given by the marshal and the minister of colonies, the duke proposed the toast: "The Franco-British Entente and the prosperity of France and her Colonial Empire." Speaking slowly but without hesitation, he said: "Our two Colonial Empires

A bouquet for the Duchess.

adjoin all over the globe ... our common frontiers, far from creating causes of dissension, encourage us towards an ever friendlier co-operation." His speech reflects the fact that while public interest in republican France is centred on the personalities of the royals in their midst there is a serious political reason behind their visit. The old empires are changing. India is growing restive and the Statute of Westminster formally confining the crown's role to a symbolic one within the dominions of a free commonwealth will become law by the end of the year. The French are facing similar demands for freedom among their colonies and in a world in the grip of economic crisis, combined with the rise of fascism, the cheers that greet Bertie and Elizabeth have a political as well as popular significance.

In Bonnie Scotland to celebrate her parents' golden anniversary

Glamis, 10 August 1931

The Yorks have travelled to Scotland to take part in the golden wedding celebrations of the duchess's parents, the Earl and Countess of Strathmore, and they have been swept into the heart of this large rumbustious family. Glamis Castle, renowned for its blood-soaked role in Scottish history, echoes with children's laughter as Princess Elizabeth and her cousins play in the ancient rooms. There is to be a grand ball, the beacon will be lit and people are arriving from all over Scotland to pay their respects to the Earl, a respected and dutiful Lord Lieutenant, and his artistic wife, Nina Cecilia. Being "royal" makes little impression on the Scots and the Yorks love it.

The Duke and Duchess with Elizabeth and her cousin Diana at Glamis Castle.

Duchess fishes for champagne while unemployed march for food

Ascot, 7 November 1931

The economic crisis is hitting hard, especially among the working class where crushing poverty adds to the humiliation of being unemployed. Only the rich seem able to continue their carefree lifestyles and even their acts of charity seem more patronising than charitable. The Duchess of York is playing a full part in raising money for the various charities in which she is involved but "fishing" for champagne hardly seems to strike the right note. What the unemployed want is work so

that they can feed their own families and they are on the march all over the country to demand jobs.

The national government is taking stringent measures to cope with the crisis. It has imposed higher taxes, curbs on spending and pay cuts on everyone over whom it has control. The king has decided that the royal family cannot be exempt and has cut the civil list payments to the family by £50,000 a year while the crisis lasts. He has given up his shooting in Windsor Great Park. The Prince of Wales, called to the

telephone in a Paris night club by the king who demanded that he join the economy drive, is relinquishing £10,000 from his estates. And here, at the bloodstock sales today, the Duke of York, near to tears, has sold his beloved hunters. He has written sorrowfully to the Master of the Pytchley, Ronald Tree: "It has come as a great shock to me that with the economy ... my hunting should have been one of the things I must do without. And I must sell my horses too. The parting with them will be terrible."

Elizabeth at charity fete in London.

Protesting unemployed workers take the low road from Scotland to the capital.

Duchess in Wales to meet the miners

Wales, April 1933
The Duchess of York is busy mending fences with the Welsh miners who are still bitter after the defeat of their long strike. She visited the hospital at Aberdare and met the miners and their pit ponies at Abercynon colliery, working her charm on men who it was feared would bring Red revolution to Britain only a few years ago. Her visit is one of a series she and the duke are making to industrial areas as the country slowly fights its way out of the grip of the Depression.

She is finding, somewhat to her surprise, that despite the hardships, there is still a great affection for the

A miner at the Abercynon colliery shows Elizabeth his Davey safety lamp during her visit to the mine.

royal family among the working class. In fact, the most dangerous opposition to the monarchy and its institutions is coming not from the poor people but from the young men and women of the professional class. Many of them, appalled by the slaughter of the world war and the rise of fascism in Europe, are turning to communism as the only hope for the future. In February of this year the nation was shocked when the Oxford Union carried by 275 votes to 153 a motion declaring that "this House will in no circumstances fight for its King and Country." None of this seems to affect the duchess as she continues her travels around the country on her official duties, meeting all sorts of people and making friends everywhere she goes whatever their class.

1934 - 1935

16 Jan 1934. Winston Churchill in a broadcast says: "We have never been so defenceless as we are now."

24 Feb 1934. Sir Edward Elgar, composer of the "Enigma Variations" and the "Pomp and Circumstance" marches, dies aged 76.

1 March 1934. Japan appoints the former Chinese emperor, Pu-Yi, as its puppet Emperor of Manchukuo.

20 June 1934. The Prince of Wales, increasingly dominated by Mrs Simpson, has severed contact with Freda Dudley Ward, his closest friend and adviser for 16 years.

30 June 1934. Hitler mounts "Night of Long Knives" against his Brownshirt stormtroopers, previously his most loyal supporters. Hundreds are murdered.

25 July 1934. Austrian Chancellor Engelbert Dolfuss is murdered in his office by a gang of Nazis in an attempted coup.

9 Oct 1934. King Alexander of Yugoslavia and French Foreign Minister Louis Barthou are assassinated in Marseilles by a Croatian nationalist.

4 March 1935. Britain increases defence spending to meet the threat of massive German rearmament.

19 May 1935. Colonel T.E. Lawrence, *Lawrence of Arabia*, dies after five days in a coma following a motor-cycle crash.

7 June 1935. The king calls on Stanley Baldwin to become prime minister again following the resignation of Ramsay MacDonald for health reasons.

19 Sept 1935. Under Hitler's Nuremberg decrees Jews are deprived of German citizenship and are banned from public life.

2 Oct 1935. Mussolini's long-expected invasion of Abyssinia began at dawn today with bombing raids as 100,000 troops crossed the border.

8 Oct 1935. Clement Attlee, a middle-class Fabian, is elected to succeed George Lansbury as leader of the Labour Party.

6 Nov 1935. The Duke of Gloucester marries Lady Alice Montagu-Douglas-Scott, daughter of the Duke of Buccleuch. The king writes in his diary: "Now all the children are married except David."

31 Dec 1935. Scientist Robert Watson-Watt has patented a method of detecting aeroplanes by reflecting radio waves off them.

Prince involved with an American divorcee

The Prince of Wales at a Pilgrim's dinner with Stanley Baldwin.

London, December 1934
The Prince of Wales is causing scandal throughout London and turmoil in the royal family by his blatant affair with Mrs Wallis Simpson, an American divorcee who is still married to her second husband. The Prince is besotted with her and caused grave offence when he presented her and her husband to the king and queen at the Buckingham Palace ball on 27 November to celebrate the marriage of the Duke of Kent to Princess Marina of Greece. There was no invitation for the Simpsons when the Yorks gave an eve-of-wedding lunch the following day. The duchess, who got on quite well with her brother-in-law's previous mistress, Thelma Furness, is bitterly opposed to Mrs Simpson because of the worry the affair is causing the ailing king and the burden it is putting on her husband's shoulders. He, in turn, is worried by the effect of the scandal on his father. Meanwhile, the infatuated prince publicly flaunts his love for Mrs Simpson while she "queens it" over their alternative court.

Duke of Kent weds Marina of Greece

London, 29 November 1934
Prince George, created Duke of Kent last month, married the stunning Princess Marina of Greece in Westminster Abbey today. The king and queen are delighted with the match, for Marina, apart from her beauty, has a reputation for being level-headed, just the sort of wife George needs since he has come close to disaster, toying with drugs and conducting a series of unsuitable affairs. It appears, however, that he has fallen in love with Marina and has reformed. The ceremony today was conducted by the Archbishop of Canterbury with a Greek Orthodox bishop in attendance. The Prince of Wales was best man, Princess Elizabeth was a bridesmaid and the royal families of Britain and Greece faced one another across the chancel. The wedding party then returned to Buckingham Palace where a Greek wedding ceremony was held in the private chapel.

Mrs Simpson at her first marriage.

Two sisters out and about in London

Arriving at Olympia for the Royal Tournament, the Services' annual display.

London, July 1935
Princess Elizabeth and Princess Margaret Rose are being shown life outside the confines of the royal family. Their governess "Crawfie" has taken them on expeditions to department stores and down the Underground but they are so popular they are usually recognised and mobbed by admiring crowds. So now their mother has begun to take them along to public events such as the Royal Tournament at Olympia where the armed forces display their skill at arms. But, however "ordinary" the occasion the duchess insists that her daughters should be dressed, and behave, like princesses because, she insists, "that's what the people expect of us".

Cheers and tears for the Silver Jubilee

On their way to St Paul's by coach for the Jubilee thanksgiving service.

London, 6 May 1935
King George and Queen Mary were given an astonishing welcome today as they drove to St Paul's Cathedral to celebrate their Silver Jubilee. It has not been an easy 25 years; the horror of the Great War was followed by the hardships of the Depression. There have been many tears. But today the whole nation has been celebrating, with street parties for the children and a "knees-up" for their parents. The king is surprised by the display of affection and loyalty. "But I am just an ordinary fellow," he said to the Archbishop of Canterbury who replied, "Yes, Sir, that's just it." Tonight, a crowd is singing "For He's a Jolly Good Fellow" outside the palace.

Philip of Greece acts in Macbeth

Gordonstoun, Summer 1935
Prince Philip of Greece, one of the many exiled princelings among Queen Victoria's descendants, is being brought up in Britain by his relatives, the Mountbattens. They have sent him to Gordonstoun, a progressive school in Morayshire run by the German teacher Kurt Hahn. Philip, more athlete than intellectual, recently played Donalbain in the school play, *Macbeth*.

Scottish pride: new colours for Black Watch

Glamis, 10 August 1935
The Duchess of York presented new colours to the Black Watch today to replace those the regiment lost in a disastrous fire in Dundee. Her daughters and husband watched as the soldiers, kilts swinging and pipes skirling, paraded in the grounds of Glamis Castle. The duchess is proud of her association with the regiment, one of the British army's most distinguished fighting units. Formed to keep watch on rebel highlanders in 1735, it recruits its men from the country around Glamis and it was with the Black Watch that the duchess's brother, Fergus, died at the battle of Loos. The duke wore the dark kilt which gave the Black Watch its name. A stickler for military protocol, his turn-out could not be faulted, down to the *skean dhu* – the black knife in his sock. Thrifty Scotswomen noted with approval that the duchess and her daughters were wearing the same clothes they had worn to the Royal Tournament earlier in the year.

Princess shows her love of horses

London, Summer 1935
Princess Elizabeth has inherited a love of horses from her mother, and they like nothing better than a horse show. The duchess learnt to ride on rough ponies in the open country round Glamis, but "Lilibet" has been taking more formal riding lessons since she was three when she was given a tiny pony as a Christmas present by King George. She has become an accomplished rider.

Philip kitted up for the school play.

At Glamis Castle for the presentation of new colours to the family regiment.

At the Richmond Horse Show.

19 Jan 1936. Rudyard Kipling, the most popular author of his day and "Poet of the Empire", dies at 70.

21 Jan 1936. The Prince of Wales, known to the royal family as David, is proclaimed King Edward VIII.

7 March 1936. The German army defies the Treaties of Versailles and Locarno and marches into the Rhineland.

8 April 1936. Horror grows at use of poison gas by the Italians in Abyssinia.

16 July 1936. As the king rides back to Buckingham Palace after presenting new colours to six Guards battalions, Scottish journalist George McMahon draws a revolver but is disarmed by a policeman before he can fire.

17 July 1936. General Francisco Franco, Spain's commander in Morocco, heads an army rebellion against the Republican government.

16 August 1936. Germany stages the Olympic Games in Berlin. Hitler is furious when American negro Jesse Owens is star of the games, winning four gold medals.

11 Oct 1936. There are fierce clashes in the East End of London when anti-fascists attempt to halt a march by 7,000 black-shirted supporters of Sir Oswald Mosley.

30 Nov 1936. The Crystal Palace, London's great showplace, is destroyed in a spectacular blaze that could be seen by airline pilots halfway to France.

29 Jan 1937. Stalin continues his purges and show trials. Thirteen former Bolshevik leaders are sentenced to death after "confessing" to high treason and conspiring with Trotsky to overthrow Stalin.

27 April 1937. The German air force, fighting for Franco, carries out a massive raid on Guernica, cultural and spiritual home of the Basques.

6 May 1937. The giant airship *Hindenburg* explodes in a ball of fire as it comes in to land in New Jersey. Thirty-three passengers and crew die.

28 May 1937. Neville Chamberlain takes over as prime minister from the retiring Stanley Baldwin.

30 August 1937. American Joe Louis beats Britain's Tommy Farr in his first heavyweight title defence at Madison Square Garden.

King George V dies and the people

The King's body borne on a gun-carriage is pulled by sailors on his last journey through his capital.

Windsor, 28 January 1936

King George V, much loved by his people, was buried in St George's Chapel here today in the presence of his family and a sombre array of mourners which included five foreign monarchs. In death he was late for possibly the only time in his adult life, the funeral being delayed for an hour by the press of the crowd on the road from the station. His coffin was lowered into the family vault and the new king, Edward VIII, sprinkled it with earth from a silver bowl. Thus ended a week of royal ritual following the death of the gruff sailor king. He was obviously frail, chronic bronchitis making every breath a struggle, when the family gathered at Sandringham for their traditional Christmas. It was not a happy occasion. Apart from his illness, the Duchess of York caught influenza which rapidly developed into pneumonia and the Prince of Wales was fretting, anxious to be with Mrs Simpson. On 16 January the Duke of York received a message from his mother asking him to return to Sandringham to help with a house party because the king was unwell and had retired to his bedroom. It then became obvious the king was dying. He did his duty to the very end. At 12.15 pm on 20 January he received three cabinet ministers to approve the formation of a Council of State to act on his behalf. He signed his initials and the ministers left in tears. A few hours later his doctor, Lord Dawson, issued a bulletin announcing: "The King's life is moving peacefully to its close." He died at five minutes to midnight with his sons and daughter at his bedside. When Lord Dawson confirmed that he was dead, Queen Mary, regal as ever, turned to the Prince of Wales and stooped to kiss his hand in homage. He was now The King of England. It was his succession to the throne that had worried his father in his last hours. He had told Prime Minister Baldwin that "after I am dead the boy will ruin himself in twelve months". And a court official had heard him say, "I pray to God that my eldest son will never marry and have children, and that nothing will come between Bertie and Lilibet and the throne".

Duchess of York arrives to join the family in escorting the coffin to London.

mourn the shy sailor king they had come to love

The royal brothers walk behind their father's coffin in his funeral cortege.

Prince of Wales leads the mourners as his father is buried in the family vault.

London, 28 January 1936
Over a million people filed past the coffin of King George as he lay in state in Westminster Hall, and there is genuine grief at his death throughout the land. As he had learnt during his Silver Jubilee celebrations, the people of Britain had come to love him. Essentially a shy man, who found it difficult to express his own feelings, he could not understand why his people should feel affection for him. "I am only a naval officer," he once said, "I just do my duty." It was precisely because he was an obviously decent man doing his best in troubled times that the nation took him to its heart. Perhaps his greatest achievement was in holding the monarchy together when so many dynasties were collapsing in Europe. No lover of change, his sense of duty led him to accept a Labour government, to urge moderation during the general strike and to seek national unity during the economic crisis. A tyrant to his family, he was a gentle ruler of his people.

In an ancient ceremony, the Heralds proclaim the Prince of Wales as the new King from the balcony of St James's Palace. He becomes King Edward VIII.

Yorks strive to lead family life in growing crisis

London, 30 July 1936

The Yorks are busy attending to their royal duties. They have visited Durham and been down the appropriately named Glamis Pit at Kibblesworth where the miners received them warmly. The Court Circular is full of their appointments: the duchess opens a new nurses' home at St Mary's Hospital, attends a display of Scottish crafts and cookery, and opens a playground on the site of the old Foundling Hospital. These are not duties to set the blood racing, but she carries them out without a hint that they are not the most important events in her life. The duke, growing in confidence and popularity, is also becoming expert at the tricks of the royal trade. At the same time they are trying to lead a cosy family life, gardening in old clothes at The Royal Lodge with their daughters joining in, and playing with their pets, a family of golden labradors and the Welsh corgis, Jane and Dookie. In the evening they entertain quietly, dine with friends and go to the theatre. The young princesses attend to their lessons, and spend much of their time playing "house" in a miniature thatched cottage given to them by the people of Wales. Elizabeth has already been introduced to royal duties, awarding the prizes to the junior competitors at the Richmond Horse Show.

They are a happy family leading a comfortable life and yet everything they do is overshadowed by the crisis which is swiftly building round

A contented family: happy with their children and their dogs, Bertie and Elizabeth continue to carry out their duties.

the reign of King Edward – "Uncle David" to the princesses. The new king has made it plain that he is bored by court life and has adopted a cavalier attitude to his duties. He has embarrassed the government by making no secret of his admiration for Hitler's National Socialist party. And, above all, he is so preoccupied by his affair with Mrs Simpson that nothing else seems to matter to him. He has abandoned caution. When

he was proclaimed king he arranged for her to watch the ceremony from a room at St James's and, contrary to all precedent, stood in the window with her to watch his own proclamation – and was photographed talking to her. At an official Buckingham Palace dinner earlier this month at which Mrs Simpson acted as the king's hostess, Mr Winston Churchill, in mischievous mood, introduced the subject of George IV

and his secret wife, Mrs Fitzherbert. The Duchess of York froze him. "Well, that," she said, "was a *long* time ago." Her sensitivity stems from the king's insistence on publishing Mrs Simpson's name in the Court Circular when announcing his guest lists. The duchess feels that she and her husband and the other guests are being used to give respectability to the king's relationship with Mrs Simpson.

At a County Durham pithead before going down the mineshaft.

With Princess Elizabeth and Princess Margaret and their family pets.

Attends prize-giving at the St John ambulance and nursing competition.

With young patient at opening of nurses' home at St Mary's Hospital.

Scandal follows Edward's cruise with Mrs Simpson

The King, Mrs Simpson and Mrs Herman Rogers during the Nahlin cruise.

Edward shows his boredom during a Buckingham Palace garden party.

Aberdeen, 24 September 1936

The king has scandalised Scotland and brought relations with the Duke and Duchess of York to breaking point with an act of crass insensitivity. Pleading that he was still in official court mourning for his father, he declined to open the new Aberdeen Infirmary yesterday, his place being taken by the duke and duchess who performed the ceremony with their customary smiling efficiency. The king, meanwhile, had driven to Aberdeen Station from Balmoral to pick up Mrs Simpson. He had the misfortune to be seen by a photographer, and this morning a picture of him wearing motoring goggles is printed alongside that of the duke and duchess carrying out their official duties. The headline reads: His Majesty In Aberdeen, Surprise Visit To Meet Guests.

The question now is: how long can the Mrs Simpson scandal be kept from the British public? Only a week ago the king returned from a cruise on board the yacht *Nahlin* with Mrs Simpson and a group of friends. From the moment the king boarded the yacht at the Yugoslav port of Sibenik on 10 August the cruise attracted worldwide interest. American reporters followed them around the Adriatic to Greece and Turkey. Crowds cheered members of the party when they went ashore and greeted the king with ribald shouts. He made no attempt to hide his closeness to Mrs Simpson. They were photographed together, swimming, sightseeing, and once with her resting her hand on his arm as he looked at her, full of affection.

The extraordinary thing is that while the rest of the world has been wallowing in the details of the cruise, the British public so far knows nothing about it. A self-imposed censorship by Fleet Street, got up by the press barons, Lord Beaverbrook and Lord Rothermere, has meant that not a word of this has reached British readers. But this is a situation that cannot last; the news is trickling in from abroad and royal circles and politicians are taking up positions for and against the king. The American press is forecasting that he will marry "Wally". The Duchess of York refuses to speak to Mrs Simpson. It cannot last. The scandal must break soon.

Press baron Lord Rothermere.

Press baron Lord Beaverbrook.

Glorious bouquet for Elizabeth

London, July 1936

The Duchess of York, a keen gardener who likes to surround herself with masses of flowers, receives bouquets wherever she goes but few are as splendid as the one she was given at British Industries House where she inspected a display of Scottish products ranging from woollens to haggis. She received it with delight, admiring the flowers and their arrangement. She would have reacted in exactly the same fashion, however, if it had been a bunch of sweet peas picked from a cottage garden. It is said of her that whenever she is given a bouquet she takes it as though she had never been given flowers in her life before, so surprised and delighted she seems. In fact, attending flower shows are among the duties she likes most of all; she discusses horticulture with considerable expertise and is particularly knowledgeable about roses. Once when asked to name her favourite flower, she replied, "All flowers." She shares her love of gardens with her husband, and they have transformed the overrun grounds of The Royal Lodge into an elegantly casual vista of grassland, shrubs and trees with hidden flower gardens and sweet-smelling herbs.

At British Industries House.

Edward angers politicians by saying 'Something must be done'

King Edward walks among local schoolboys at Dynas during his controversial tour of distressed areas in South Wales.

South Wales, 19 November 1936

King Edward completed his tour of the depressed areas of South Wales today. He has been shocked by the scale of unemployment in the mining valleys. "Something must be done to find them work," he told an official at one point. The king was cheered throughout his two-day visit which clearly left him profoundly moved by the loyalty he was shown despite the poverty of the people. At Dowlais hundreds of men greeted him by singing an old Welsh hymn amongst the debris of the derelict Dowlais Steel Works which once made some of the finest steel in the empire. Putting aside his own troubles, he spoke to men who have been out of work for years. Short of food, with no money to clothe their families and no chance of jobs, these men, so like the soldiers he had met in the war, brought out the best in the king. At Pontypool he told a crowd: "You may be sure that all I can do for you I will." Later, at Blaenavon, in Gwent, he returned to this theme: "Something will be done about employment." This was a different king to the bored man of the garden parties and the uncaring pleasure-seeker of the *Nahlin*, and

the people responded enthusiastically to him, with miners rushing from their pit, black with coal dust, to welcome him. However, his sincerity and determination that something must be done seem likely to add to his problems for his remarks are being construed as an attack on the government and a blatant involvement in politics, far beyond his constitutional powers. Some observers feel that the king will soon lose interest when he returns to London and is once again pre-occupied with Mrs Simpson. Others fear that with Prime Minister Stanley Baldwin's refusal to meet the Jarrow unemployed marchers because "this is the way in which civil strife begins and civil strife may not end until it is civil war," the king may appeal to the people over the head of the government in any confrontation about Mrs Simpson.

The King inspects members of the British Legion on parade at Pontypool.

Elizabeth fears for family future

London, 2 December 1936

As each day passes and the constitutional crisis grows ever more serious, the Duchess of York is facing the fact that her cosy family life might soon be ended and that she and her husband and daughters will be asked to fulfil roles they have never wanted and have never been trained to carry out. If the king abdicates they will become king and queen and Princess Elizabeth will become the heir apparent. It is a frightening prospect and it is made no easier by the strain it is putting on her husband. The king is refusing to see him and will not answer his telephone calls. The duchess is furious with the king for treating her husband in this fashion and the steel in her character is showing through the velvet. Implacable towards Mrs Simpson, who contemptuously refers to her as "Cookie", she marks down the king's supporters as her enemies. These include powerful men such as Winston Churchill and Lord Beaverbrook who are trying to keep Edward on the throne by allowing him to contract a morganatic marriage with Mrs Simpson. The tide is running against them, however, and it grows ever more likely that "Cookie" will be queen.

In the security of Glamis Castle.

Scandal! Mrs Simpson flees to France

After months of rumour and cover up the constitutional crisis threatens to force King Edward VIII from the throne.

London, 3 December 1936

The people of Britain know today what the rest of the world has known for months: their king is in love with the twice-divorced American, Wallis Simpson, and is prepared to abdicate if he cannot marry her and remain king. The gag on the press instituted by Lord Beaverbrook and Lord Rothermere can no longer be sustained, the long-awaited storm has broken and Mrs Simpson has fled to France to escape the turmoil.

The tragedy became inevitable on 27 October when Mrs Simpson filed for divorce at Ipswich, prompting headlines in the American press such as "King's Moll Reno'd in Wolsey's Home Town". Then, on 16 November, on the eve of his visit to Wales, the king told his family and the Prime Minister Stanley Baldwin of his intention to marry Mrs Simpson when her divorce becomes absolute and that he would rather give up the throne than the woman he loves. He summoned the prime minister to Buckingham Palace to tell him of his intentions and Baldwin informed him that his decision was "very grave" for he doubted if the country and the commonwealth would ac-

cept such a marriage. The king then broke the news to his mother and sister over dinner and Queen Mary urged him to put his duty to his country before his personal wishes, and she icily refused his request that she receive Mrs Simpson.

On 27 November the prime minister told the cabinet of his intention to ask the leaders of the dominions for their views on the constitutional

crisis. But it was a sermon by the Bishop of Bradford, commenting on the king's need to show more awareness of his Christian duty, that set off the storm. The press could ignore the crisis no longer. Their tone is critical and the reporting has dismayed the king who thought that his popularity with the people would triumph over the disapproval of the government and his family.

The lovers: Wallis and Edward.

Edward showers Wallis with jewels. ▷

King Edward abdicates! He tells the nation that

London, 10 December 1936

King Edward VIII, determined to marry Mrs Simpson against the advice of the government, the church and the leaders of the dominions, today took the only course open to him: he abdicated from the throne which he ascended on the death of his father on January 20. The drama came to its climax this morning at Buckingham Palace when he signed an Instrument of Abdication, just two paragraphs long in which he declared his "irrevocable determination to renounce the Throne for myself and for my descendants".

Prime Minister Baldwin carried the Instrument to the House of Commons where it was read by the Speaker to a packed, solemn chamber. The Speaker also read the king's last message to the house in which he said: "The burden which constantly rests upon the shoulders of a Sovereign is so heavy that it can only be borne in circumstances different from those in which I now find myself. I am conscious that I can no longer discharge this heavy task with efficiency or with satisfaction to myself." Immediately after the Speaker had read the message Mr Baldwin rose to move that it be considered. "No more grave message has ever been received by Parliament," he said, "and no more difficult and, I might almost say, more repugnant task has ever been imposed on a Prime Minister."

The king has not been without his supporters. He remains popular with the public and crowds have gathered in Downing Street carry-

King Edward makes his abdication speech from Windsor Castle before leaving the country to join Mrs Simpson.

ing placards proclaiming "God Save The King From Baldwin" and "We want King Edward". Lord Beaverbrook has sought desperately to find ways of keeping him on the throne but in the end even Beaverbrook has had to give up, telling Churchill, "Our cock won't fight." They are among the politicians who fear the Duke of York will never be strong

enough to be king – a task he is reluctant to undertake. There has been a move to bypass him and give the crown to the younger, more robust Duke of Kent. But Kent has been involved in drug-taking and there are rumours about his sexuality and this move also failed. What has told in the Duke of York's favour is the evident suitability of his wife to

be consort despite the smart set's sneers at "the little duchess". It was not, however, until three days ago that the king told Bertie that he planned to abdicate and that he was to be the new king. Bertie broke down and wept like a child. He then went home to Elizabeth, who, laid low by influenza, has been unable to lend him her customary support.

Prime Minister Baldwin leaves No 10 Downing Street to report to Parliament.

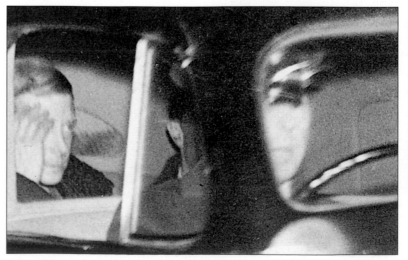

Edward leaves his castle. No longer king, he is now the Duke of Windsor.

he cannot live without the woman he loves

One of the king's loyal subjects ...

... shows his support all round town.

London, 12 December 1936

The former King Edward VIII, now the Duke of Windsor, slipped away from England into exile in the early hours of this morning on board the destroyer HMS *Fury*. Earlier, introduced by Sir John Reith as "His Royal Highness, Prince Edward" he had made an emotional broadcast from Windsor Castle to the nation explaining why he had abdicated. "I have for twenty-five years tried to serve," he said, "but you must believe me when I tell you that I have found it impossible to carry the heavy burden of responsibility and to discharge my duties as king as I would wish to do without the help and support of the woman I love ... God bless you all. God save the King." He went on to pledge allegiance to the new king and acknowledged the stability and strength that Elizabeth had brought to his brother: "He has one matchless blessing, enjoyed by so many of you and not bestowed on me – a happy home with his wife and children."

After the broadcast he drank a whisky and soda and drove to the York's house where he had dined with his family before the broadcast and they had remained to say goodbye to him. The Princess Royal wept, Queen Mary was as imperious as ever, and his brothers chattered aimlessly about everything except his departure. Eventually, with the night growing late and foggy, he said his goodbyes, bowing over the new king's hand in an act of homage, then climbed into his Daimler and vanished into the gloom. He is to go to Austria while Mrs Simpson stays at a friend's villa in Cannes until her divorce is made absolute in the next couple months and they are free to marry.

The former Duke and Duchess of York are finding it difficult to comprehend that they are now the King and Queen of Great Britain. The queen, still recovering from the flu, has written to the Archbishop of Canterbury: "I can hardly now believe that we have been called to this tremendous task and the curious thing is that we aren't afraid. I feel that God has enabled us to face the situation calmly." Over lunch Bertie asks his wife: "If someone should come through on the telephone, who should I say I am?"

Duke of Kent: a possible successor?

Winston Churchill attends the Accession Council to proclaim Bertie king.

That question was settled today at a meeting of the Accession Council at St James's Palace where he was proclaimed King George VI. He took the Oath of Accession and told the council: "With my wife and helpmeet by my side I take up the heavy task which lies before me." His wife will be the first Queen Elizabeth since Elizabeth Tudor, 1588 to 1603, and the first Scottish queen since Mary, Queen of Scots, who was sent to the execution block by Elizabeth I in 1587. Curiously, the people's support for Edward has quickly begun to wane with his departure. They, too, believe in a happy home with a wife and children.

The ladies demonstrating their heart-felt affection for the former king.

Ideals and bullets in Spain's Civil War

Madrid, 20 December 1936

The Civil War in Spain is starting to involve the rest of the world. Idealists from many countries who see the war as the first test of strength between fascism and communism are making their way to the Spanish battlefields. Most of them are joining the International Brigade engaged in the Republicans' defence of Madrid against General Francisco Franco's Nationalist army. This brigade, although organised and led by communists, is not entirely communist and has attracted young men and women from all walks of life who are against fascism. Opposing them are other equally dedicated young people convinced that they must prevent the spread of communism. But behind their idealism lurks big power intervention. Russia is supporting the Republicans while Germany and Italy have sent men, ships and aircraft to help Franco. It is beginning to look like a rehearsal for a world-wide conflict of ideologies.

Bertie and Elizabeth, the reluctant monarchs, are

London, 12 May 1937

On this, the day originally chosen for the coronation of abdicated King Edward VIII, King George VI and Queen Elizabeth were crowned in Westminster Abbey with all the pomp and ceremony of this time-honoured tradition. The people have taken their reluctant monarch and his wife to their hearts and there has been a tremendous air of excitement in the capital for days as people prepared street parties and secured their vantage points along the route.

At 10.30 this morning the king and queen left Buckingham Palace for the abbey in the State Coach, all glass and gold, drawn by a team of Windsor Greys through the cheering throngs. It was a splendid sight with four postilions and six footmen plus eight grooms and four Yeomen of the Guard walking alongside. The king wore robes of deep red and snow-white ermine with the historic Cap of Maintenance on his head, and the queen, smiling and seemingly relaxed, was dressed in a gown of ivory satin embroidered in pure gold thread with the emblems of the British Isles and the Dominions.

All went well, despite some rain, until they reached the abbey when an elderly cleric fainted just as the queen, her 18-foot train of purple velvet carried by six maids of honour, set off up the nave. Everything

The royal family pose in their coronation robes after the abbey ceremony.

was delayed, with the king growing visibly more nervous, until the cleric could be moved. As the new queen passed the royal box where Queen Mary stood with Princess Elizabeth and Princess Margaret Rose, the old queen curtsied. She had broken tradition, for previously queen dowagers have not attended the coronation of their successors. Many saw her gesture as a mark of support for her son and his wife who have come to the throne in such extraordinary and unwanted circumstances.

Then came the first words in the long service, every action of which is imbued with historic symbolism. Dr Cosmo Lang, Archbishop of Canterbury declared: "Sirs, I here present to you King George, your undoubted king ... " The congregation, filling every part of the abbey, responded in unison, shouting: "God Save King George." When it was all over the trumpets sounded, the processions reformed and their Majesties drove back to Buckingham Palace to the sound of pealing bells. Later, the royal party, still wearing their robes and crowns, appeared on the balcony to accept the acclamation of the people. There may still be some doubts about Bertie's fitness to be king but the semi-mystical ceremony of the coronation, heard for the first time by millions on their wireless sets, means that he is, indeed, their "undoubted king".

The new Queen, smiling shyly on the Balcony of Buckingham Palace.

Queen Mary looks after Elizabeth and the bored Margaret at the coronation.

crowned King and Queen in Westminster Abbey

The royal family, all wearing their crowns, gathers on the balcony of Buckingham Palace to greet the cheering crowds who are celebrating their coronation.

The procession passes through Trafalgar Square on its way to the abbey.

Ex-King Edward weds his beloved Wallis

Tours, France, 3 June 1937
The Duke of Windsor has finally married the woman for whom he renounced the crown. At the Château de Candé near here today, Wallis Warfield – she had resumed her original name – became the Duchess of Windsor. She will not, however, be known as "Her Royal Highness". Months of negotiation have failed to sway the king who argued that to make her "HRH" would be to accept her into the royal family which was impossible. The duke was furious when he was told of the king's decision. "This is a fine wedding present," he said. The rift between the brothers who were once so close grows ever wider. They have haggled over the duke's financial settlement and the king forbade other members of the royal family to attend the wedding. The queen has fully supported her husband in his attitude towards the new duchess whose influence she fears. But at least the marriage was conducted by Anglican rites: a publicity-seeking clergyman from Darlington conducted the service.

The Duke of Windsor and his bride.

57

22 Oct 1937. The Duke and Duchess of Windsor, who are visiting Berlin to "study social conditions and housing problems", are fulsomely welcomed by Hitler.

16 Nov 1937. The House of Commons votes in favour of building air raid shelters in most of Britain's towns and cities.

3 Jan 1938. Government announces that all children are to be issued gas masks.

14 Jan 1938. Walt Disney's first feature-length cartoon, *Snow White and the Seven Dwarfs* is a world-wide success.

21 Feb 1938. Anthony Eden resigns as Foreign Secretary over what he considers is Chamberlain's appeasement of Hitler and Mussolini.

14 March 1938. Adolf Hitler celebrates his bloodless acquisition of Austria by driving into Vienna today to a tumultuous welcome and declares: "the German nation will never again be rent apart."

15 March 1938. One of the most sensational of the Moscow show trials has ended with the execution of 18 high-ranking Soviet leaders, including Nikolai Bukharin, the "darling" of the Bolshevik Party.

24 March 1938. Mr Chamberlain tells Parliament that Britain is ready to go to war to defend France and Belgium but is not automatically committed to protect Czechoslovakia.

19 April 1938. General Franco's troops win a stunning victory in Catalonia, cutting Republican Spain in two.

25 April 1938. The Baptist Union condemns the "phenomenal growth" of football pools as "injurious to moral sense and healthy sport".

10 May 1938. Thomas Cook is offering eight days on the Riviera this summer for £8/17/6d.

14 May 1938. England's footballers give the Nazi salute before playing the Germans in Berlin. England wins 6-3.

8 June 1938. Japanese planes have bombed Canton mercilessly for the past 10 days. The city is a smoking ruin and thousands have been killed.

24 June 1938. The RAF launches a new recruitment campaign; it receives 1,000 inquiries on the first day.

30 June 1938. A new comic has been launched in New York; it is called "Superman".

Hitler demands more living space

Nuremberg, 6 September 1937
Chancellor Adolf Hitler, in a powerful speech at the annual Nazi rally which brings his storm troopers here in their thousands to take part in militaristic torchlit parades, has renewed his demand for more "lebensraum" (living room). He said that "without colonies Germany's space is too small to guarantee that our people can be fed safely and continuously. The attitude of other powers to our demand is simply incomprehensible." He called on those "other powers" to read the signs of the times. He gave no indication if he was referring to Germany's old colonies in Africa or to the lands across Germany's eastern border which he threatened to seize in his book, *Mein Kampf*.

Queen honors the dead on Armistice Day

The Queen attends the service of remembrance at the Cenotaph.

London, 11 November 1937
The king and queen today attended the service of remembrance to honour the dead of the Great War at the Cenotaph. The queen watched as her husband laid his wreath of poppies and then, when the buglers sounded the Last Post, they joined the nation in the minute's silence to mark the eleventh hour on the eleventh day of the eleventh month when the shooting stopped. Tears formed in her eyes; no doubt she was remembering her brother, Fergus, who died in the war. She grew close to the wounded soldiers she entertained at Glamis and her empathy with the old soldiers was obvious when, the service over, the bands played and they swung down Whitehall, civilians now but marching in step and wearing their medals with pride.

The Scottish Queen of England is welcomed by her countrymen

The princesses admire the eagles' feathers of the Royal Company of Archers, their Scottish bodyguard at Holyrood.

Glasgow, 3 May 1938
The king and queen were given a rapturous reception when they opened the Empire Exhibition at Bellahouston Park today. There was a particularly warm welcome for Queen Elizabeth, who was presented with the badge of the Order of the Thistle, Scotland's highest order of chivalry, by the exhibition's president, Lord Elgin. The royal couple went up the Empire Tower in a lift that moves at 500 feet a minute and spent five hours touring the exhibition's displays. Their visit ended at the North Hillingdon estate where 1,400 men are turning farmland into a modern industrial estate.

Romantic visit for the King and Queen

The King and Queen walk with her brother David at St Paul's Walden Bury.

Walden Bury, Spring 1938
The king and queen have been visiting St Paul's Walden Bury, the Hertfordshire home of the Bowes Lyon family. It is a place of happy memories for them both for it was here that Lady Elizabeth spent much of her childhood when she was not at Glamis, and it was in its wooded grounds that Bertie eventually persuaded her to marry him. The Queen Anne house, known to the family as "The Bury", has been inherited by David, the youngest of the Bowes Lyon children and the companion of the queen's early years. It is ideal for him, accessible to his work in the City, and with ample grounds for him to exercise his interest in horticulture.

New colours for the Grenadier Guards

Buckingham Palace, May 1938
The royal ladies gathered in the spring sunshine today to watch the king present new colours to the Grenadier Guards. The queen, the two little princesses, Queen Mary and the Princess Royal observed from the palace steps as the Grenadiers, resplendent in their red tunics and bearskins, drilled as only guardsmen can. The colours, round which a regiment rallies in the fog of battle, may have no place on the modern battlefield but the symbolism of today's ceremony is particularly apt as Britain hurries to re-arm to face the threat posed by the fascist dictators. Last month Hitler annexed Austria and is now making threatening noises towards Czechoslovakia. Earlier this month Prime Minister Neville Chamberlain bought time by an agreement with Mussolini which acknowledges Italy's annexation of Abyssinia. In a world which seems to be hurrying towards war, the ancient traditions of the British army and royal family may be needed to form a rallying point for the nation.

A royal turnout for the Guards as the fear of war continues to grow.

The Queen's much loved mother dies

London, 23 June 1938
The queen's mother, the Countess of Strathmore, died at her Mayfair home today after a long illness. She was 75 and had never really recovered from the death of her son, Fergus, in the war. She was a remarkable woman, possessing many of those qualities which are now revealing themselves in her daughter. She was a talented musician and an expert gardener and brought a sense of fun to the somewhat dour Bowes Lyon family. But she also had a keen sense of duty and impressed on her children the need for self-discipline. The queen is heart-broken by the loss of someone who set her an example all her life and to whom she could turn for wise advice untainted by court sophistries. Lady Strathmore is to be buried at Glamis where she spent so many happy days surrounded by her large family. Her death has caused diplomatic problems as well as sorrow, for the king and queen were due to start a State visit to France in five days time. It must now be postponed.

Queen Elizabeth stuns the fashionable French in her white gown

Paris, 21 July 1938
The king and queen's State visit to Paris has been a triumph. The queen, still in mourning for her mother, has stunned the fashion-conscious French with a series of dresses designed for her by Norman Hartnell in the alternative mourning colour of white. At Versailles today the king reviewed 50,000 French troops but it was the queen's romantic, frothy white dress with matching hat and parasol that brought gasps from the crowd. As one newspaper headline puts it: "We have taken the Queen to our hearts. She rules over two nations." Mme Lebrun, wife of the French president, told her: "I wish to assure Your Majesty that she has won the hearts of the whole of Paris." It seems that the French were eager to have their hearts won.

Thousands of people have poured into the capital to welcome the royal couple. The streets are garlanded with flags and bunting. The visit has achieved all that was hoped from it. New life has been breathed into the *entente cordiale* at a time when the spectre of war hovers over Europe. The reality behind the frothy white dress at Versailles is the gas masks being issued in London.

Leaving the Elysée Palace.

A garden party in Paris: the King and Queen with President Lebrun.

3 July 1938. The *Mallard*, a British steam locomotive, reaches a record 126 mph over 300 yards on a run from Newcastle to London.

15 July 1938. Tycoon aviator Howard Hughes gets a ticker tape reception after completing record round-the-world flight in three days, 19 hours and 17 minutes to publicise the New York World's Fair.

7 August 1938. The liner *Queen Mary* sets a record for the westward Atlantic crossing of three days, 23 hours and 48 minutes.

20 August 1938. Sydney Wooderson runs the half-mile in a world record time of one minute, 49.2 seconds.

24 August 1938. England batsman Len Hutton scores a record 363 runs in a Test match against Australia at the Oval. England wins by the unprecedented margin of an innings and 579 runs.

25 August 1938. Austria's former leaders are being held in Dachau concentration camp.

1 Sept 1938. Mussolini expels Jews who entered Italy after 1918.

8 Sept 1938. Germans living in Czech territory of Sudetenland hold mass rallies to demand union with Germany.

14 Sept 1938. Czechoslovakia extends martial law to the Sudetenland to quell German agitation.

25 Sept 1938. There is a rush by Londoners for gas masks as international tension escalates.

3 Oct 1938. Duff Cooper resigns as First Lord of the Admiralty over Chamberlain's appeasement of Hitler.

25 Oct 1938. The Duke of Kent is appointed Governor-General of Australia.

30 Oct 1938. Orson Welles' vivid radio production of "War of the Worlds" is so realistic that it causes widespread panic in the United States.

9 Nov 1938. Nazi thugs go on the rampage in Berlin in an orgy of anti-semitic terror called Kristallnacht because of the number of Jewish shops' windows that were smashed.

24 Nov 1938. Neville Chamberlain and French premier Daladier visit the Duke and Duchess of Windsor in Paris.

1 Dec 1938. The British government unveils plans for a "National Register" stating what to do in time of war.

Queen launches world's biggest liner

The Cunard White Star Line will operate the 'Queen Elizabeth' on the North Atlantic route with the 'Queen Mary'.

Clydebank, 27 September 1938
The queen, acting in place of the king who is too preoccupied by the worsening international situation to leave London, launched the world's largest liner here today. She gave the ship-builders of John Brown's yard a message from her husband: "He bids the people of this country to be of good cheer in spite of the dark clouds hanging over them and, indeed, over the whole world." The 80,000-ton liner nearly slid into the water unnamed when the restraining timbers gave way and, almost unnoticed, she started to move down the slipway while the queen and her daughters were chatting to shipyard executives. Realising what was happening, the queen leant forward and released the launching champagne which just reached the liner's bows as she gathered speed. As the bubbly foamed and the crowd cheered the queen said: "I name this ship *Queen Elizabeth*. God bless her and all who sail in her."

A visit to the theatre for Princess Elizabeth

Arriving at the Holborn Empire for 'Where the Rainbow Ends'.

London, December 1938
The queen and Princess Elizabeth have been to see the children's Christmas play *Where the Rainbow Ends* at the Holborn Empire. The princess, now 12, was enthralled. She and her sister are fond of play-acting and put on their own shows, noted for their enthusiasm rather than their expertise. The queen, who inherited her mother's artistic tastes, is anxious to encourage her daughters into a proper appreciation of the theatre but it would appear she is fighting a losing battle. The king prefers the musical comedies of Ivor Novello and Noel Coward to serious theatre and the princesses are showing similar inclinations. Like thousands of other children, their favourite radio programme is *Children's Hour*. Princess Margaret is already a wickedly clever mimic and is proving an apt pupil at the piano.

Windsor, Summer 1938. On parade at a rally in the Quadrangle of Windsor Palace: the two princesses have followed their mother into the Girl Guide movement; Elizabeth is a Guide and Margaret a Brownie.

Munich: Chamberlain claims 'Peace in our time'

London, 30 September 1938

Neville Chamberlain appeared on the balcony of Buckingham Palace flanked by the king and queen tonight and was given a tumultuous welcome by a huge throng of people rejoicing that he had averted the march to war in 12 hours of talks in Munich with Herr Hitler, Signor Mussolini and Monsieur Daladier. The celebrations started when he landed at Heston aerodrome and, waving a copy of the Anglo-German accord, said: "I believe it is peace for our time." Later, at No 10 Downing Street, he said that his mission had brought peace with honour. There is no doubt that most people, including the king and queen, are overjoyed that the threat of war has been lifted.

However, the solution reached at Munich will not please everyone, especially the Czechs who were not present at the conference, for it grants almost all Hitler's demands. The Sudeten region of Czechoslovakia, which is inhabited by a German-speaking minority, will be handed over to Germany. The terms of the pact stipulate that "the evacuation of the region shall be completed by Oct 10, without destruction of any of the existing installations" and "the occupation by stages of the

Prime Minister Chamberlain shows the crowd the Anglo-German accord on his return from his meeting with Hitler.

predominantly German territories by German troops will begin on Oct 1". Hitler has thus won another victory by the threat of war without going to war. Chamberlain's agreement to Czechoslovakia's dismemberment sits awkwardly with his statement on mobilising the fleet four days ago when he said: "I am a man of peace to the depths of my soul. Armed conflict between na-

tions is a nightmare to me, but if I were convinced that any nation had made up its mind to dominate the world by fear of its force I should feel it should be resisted. Under such a domination the life of people who believe in liberty would not be worth living." It remains to be seen when he believes that point will be reached. Behind the general euphoria, there's certainly a feeling among

MPs of all parties that we have sold out to Hitler and by giving in to him we have made war inevitable. Most powerful and vocal among these is Winston Churchill. Others argue that Britain's forces are so run down that the deal was necessary to buy time for the rearmament programme to be completed. For the moment, however, the nation rejoices in "peace in our time".

Londoners, grateful for peace, cheer the Prime Minister and the King.

Downing Street is besieged by throng, joyful that there will be no war.

15 Jan 1939. Charles Lindbergh is attacked by Soviet propagandists for being "Hitler's lackey".

17 Jan 1939. In Berlin, Jews are banned from being dentists, vets and pharmacists; also are prohibited to drive, go to the theatre, cinemas and concerts.

20 Jan 1939. King Farouk of Egypt is declared the Caliph, spiritual leader of Islam.

28 Jan 1939. W.B. Yeats, the voice of Ireland regarded by many as finest modern English-language poet, has died at 73.

9 Feb 1939. Air raid shelters made out of corrugated steel are being delivered to homes in districts most likely to be bombed in the event of war.

14 Feb 1939. Germany launches the 35,000-ton battleship *Bismarck*.

16 Feb 1939. The German envoy to the Vatican asks the College of Cardinals to elect a pope sympathetic to fascism to replace the anti-fascist Pope Pius XI who died last week.

28 Feb 1939. The government's recognition of General Franco causes furious scenes in the House of Commons. The opposition greets the prime minister with cries of "Heil Chamberlain".

3 March 1939. John Ford's western *Stagecoach* starring a young actor called John Wayne opens in America.

10 March 1939. Twenty IRA terrorists are jailed for 20 years for conspiring to cause explosions.

14 March 1939. Hitler enters Prague as a conqueror and raises his standard on Hradzin Castle, ancient palace of the Bohemian kings.

28 March 1939. Madrid has surrendered after a three year siege and the civil war in Spain has ended in a complete victory for General Franco.

8 April 1939. Invading Italian troops occupy the Albanian capital of Tirana. King Zog flees. Britain warns Italy not to go beyond Albania.

11 April 1939. Glasgow bans darts in pubs because they are "too dangerous".

26 April 1939. Germany sets new air speed record of 484.4 mph with a Messerschmitt fighter.

27 April 1939. House of Commons endorses the government's decision to conscript men aged 20 for military service.

French President pays a State visit

London, 24 March 1939

President and Madame Lebrun of France have enjoyed a glittering State visit to London with the king and queen making every effort to return the hospitality shown them on their triumphant visit to Paris last year. The Household Cavalry escorted the Lebruns to Buckingham Palace with the Mall fluttering with the red, white and blue flags of both nations. The French party was banqueted at the palace and returned the compliment at the French embassy. It is, of course, far more than return hospitality between two heads of state. War with Germany now seems inevitable and the *entente cordiale* first forged by the king's grandfather, Edward VII, once again becomes vital for the survival of both countries. It is expected that within the coming few days Mr Chamberlain will tell the House of Commons that Britain and France are pledged to defend Poland against German aggression.

Chamberlain, who brought back "peace in our time" from Munich in September and undertook another appeasing mission in January to Mussolini in Rome, finally had his eyes opened 10 days ago when Hitler seized what remained of Czechoslovakia. On 17 March, in a speech intended to mark his 70th birthday, he denounced Hitler and recalled the British ambassador to Berlin.

Dressed for dinner: the King and Queen arrive for French embassy banquet.

War now seems inevitable

The king and queen, who had fervently supported his efforts on his return from Munich, have also changed their minds about peace at any price and the king has written to the prime minister congratulating him on his stand against Hitler. They have their own problems with the Duke of Windsor who, after an embarrassing visit to Hitler during which he gave the Nazi salute, is now agitating to return to London and be given an "appropriate" job. The queen is rock-hard in her refusal to allow this. She fears that his old friends would form an alternative court dominated by "that woman" in opposition to her Bertie.

President Albert Lebrun and his wife say their farewells at Victoria Station.

Royal couple set sail to conquer the New World

Ottawa, 26 May 1939

The State visit by the king and queen to Canada is turning into a triumphal procession. The Canadians had been led to expect a king unable to utter a word and a plump and dowdy queen but they are seeing a charming, friendly young man and a vivacious woman with sparkling eyes and a smile for everyone. Everywhere the royal couple go they are winning the friendship of the people with their sincerity.

Here, where the king unveiled Canada's war memorial, the queen said she wanted to go among the veterans and she and her husband disappeared among the crowd of 6,000 old soldiers, many of whom were weeping with emotion. In the afternoon there was a warm farewell at the station with the band playing and the crowd singing "Will Ye No Come Back Again".

In French-speaking Quebec the crowd shouted "Vive le Roi" and "Vive la Reine." In Toronto they met the Dionne quins whose birth has made medical history and when Cecile impulsively ran across to kiss the queen, she went down on her knees to cuddle the little girl. All this has led the Governor General, Lord Tweedsmuir – the novelist John Buchan – to report to London: "Our monarchs are the most remarkable young people ... as for the queen, she has a perfect genius for the right kind of publicity, the unrehearsed episodes here were marvellous."

It could all have gone so wrong

The princesses say goodbye as their parents set out for North America.

Dedicating Canada's war memorial.

for while they were in mid-Atlantic on board the *Empress of Australia* the Duke of Windsor made an embarrassing broadcast from the battlefield of Verdun which amounted to an appeal for peace at any price and was generally regarded as an example of his susceptibility to fascism and an attempt to undermine his brother at the outset of his North American tour. It caused alarm because the tour is the most important task the royal couple have undertaken. With Hitler becoming ever more belligerent it is vital that Britain wins the support of this great dominion and the friendship of the United States with its vast industrial, economic and military potential.

Making friends with an Indian child at an encampment at Calgary, Alberta.

Queen and Prime Minister McKenzie King in full uniform for State occasion.

The King and Queen win important

New York, 11 June 1939
Tonight staunch American Republicans lined the railway track singing "Auld Lang Syne" as the king and queen, waving from the rear platform of their train, make their way back to Canada from President Roosevelt's Hyde Park estate on the Hudson River. Their visit to America has been an astonishing success. Even before they stepped out of their train at Washington's Grand Union Station four days ago, hard-bitten American reporters covering their tour of Canada had been won over by their charm and written glowing reports about them.

The king and the president, aware of the importance of the mission, quickly established a special relationship of genuine as well as political friendship. The queen and Mrs Roosevelt got on equally well and the queen established her own love affair with the American people. Even Washington's politicians fell for her with one isolationist senator congratulating the king on being a "good queen-picker". There followed a whirlwind tour in stifling heat with hardly a moment to rest. They visited the Capitol and were addressed as "Cousin George" and "Cousin Elizabeth", attended a dinner at the White House where they were entertained with cowboy songs and visited a boys' camp which the king wanted to compare with his own summer camp for boys.

'New York cheers'

Then, after a British embassy banquet, they took the night train to New York – and took the city by storm. As they drove to the World's Fair, ships sounded their sirens, Flying Fortresses flew overhead and New Yorkers turned out in their thousands to cheer. The *New York World Telegram* summed it up: "No matter what our future opinions might be about the British Empire ... there will be forever only affection for the charming pair who visited us, smilin' through." President Roosevelt insisted they spend their last night at his home and the two men, along with Canadian Prime Minister Mackenzie King, talked long into the night, sealing their friendship.

The royals and President Roosevelt drive past the Capitol in Washington.

President and Mrs Roosevelt greet the King and Queen at Union Station.

friends in America with war looming in Europe

Smiles all round: King George VI and President Roosevelt become instant friends and form a special relationship.

London, 23 June 1939

Princesses Elizabeth and Margaret Rose went aboard the liner *Empress of Britain* at Southampton yesterday to welcome their parents home after their long tour of North America. But even the warmth of the princesses' greeting did not prepare the king and queen for the rapturous welcome given them when they arrived at Buckingham Palace. It seemed that the whole of London, recognising what a triumph their tour has been for Britain, had turned out to celebrate their return. Fifty thousand people roared for them to

appear on the balcony last night, and when they did, sang the National Anthem and "For He's a Jolly Good Fellow". Then, when the royal couple eventually went in to dinner, they could hear the crowd serenading them with "The Lambeth Walk" and "Under the Spreading Chestnut Tree".

Behind the sheer pleasure of their welcome lies the knowledge that at last they have been properly accepted as king and queen. Their tour of America and Canada has made them; all doubts have been swept away. They travelled 10,000 miles

and were seen by some 15 million people, and they have done a wonderful job for their country. The visit was a gamble. The Americans, with their strong German and Irish minorities, and imbued with isola-

tionism, could have turned against them. The king might not have got on with Roosevelt. Many Americans feel that the Duke of Windsor had been forced to abdicate because he wanted to make an American his queen. There was the danger that the royal couple would be swallowed up, unnoticed, in the vast expanse of Canada. But the gamble came off.

Far from being lost on the Canadian prairie, the queen gave instructions that they were to be informed whenever people had gathered at remote settlements to greet the royal train and they always appeared on the rear platform – once with the queen wearing her dressing gown and a tiara – to wave as the train slowed to a crawl. In Washington a newspaper headline proclaimed: "The British Retake Washington". Roosevelt yelled "Godspeed" to them as they left the United States and strong men wept as they sailed for home from Halifax.

Today, they confirmed their new standing with the queen watching proudly as the king, full of confidence, reported on his tour at the Guildhall, impressing even Winston Churchill, as he spoke of the commonwealth and its ideals of liberty and justice under the threat of war.

Meeting the President's mother: on the porch at the Roosevelt estate.

Tired but triumphant, the royal couple say farewell to their new friends.

Princess Elizabeth introduced to her distant cousin Prince Philip

Dartmouth, 22 July 1939
The royal family, accompanied by Lord Mountbatten, are cruising along the south coast in the royal yacht *Victoria and Albert*. Their first stop has been at the Dartmouth Royal Naval College where the king and his cousin have enjoyed reliving memories of their time as cadets. "Dickie" Mountbatten has arranged for the two princesses to be looked after by his nephew, Prince Philip of Greece, who is 18 and approaching the end of his training at the college. It is not known if this is the first meeting between the flaxen-haired prince and his distant cousins, but Princess Elizabeth, now 13, appears to be smitten by him.

They played croquet in the garden and larked about on the tennis court and the princess was impressed by his ability to eat a mountain of shrimps followed by a banana split. Like most young men in the company of adoring younger girls, he showed off terribly but "Lilibet" loved every minute of it. Philip does not have a drop of Greek blood in him. He is a Dane and his looks

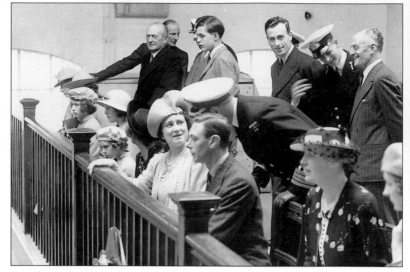
Royal family, Mountbatten and Prince Philip at Dartmouth Naval College.

betray his Viking ancestry. After the Greeks won their independence from Turkey in 1863, they searched for a European prince to become their king and, after several disappointments, Prince William of Denmark accepted the crown. Prince Philip is his descendant. Wearing the Greek crown did not have much

security of tenure and in 1922 the young Philip, in a cot made from an orange box, was rescued from revolutionaries by a British agent and the cruiser HMS *Calypso*. His father, Prince Andrew, retired to Monte Carlo and Philip was passed around his European relatives until he was taken over by "Uncle Dickie".

Awestruck children before an elegant lady

London, July 1939
The queen, her adventures in North America over, has picked up the thread of royal duties. Despite the threat of war, it is business as usual for the royal firm. Fortunate couples – but nobody who has been through the divorce courts – are invited to Buckingham Palace garden parties where they eat thin cucumber sandwiches, struggle to glimpse the king and queen, and, if they are especially privileged, will be ushered into their presence by a royal aide.

The queen is also attending less formal garden parties, charity fetes and horticultural shows but, wherever she goes, she dresses impeccably because "that is what the people expect of me". Her remarkable instinctive flair for public relations has been developed by her foreign tours and she hardly puts a foot wrong with her admiring public. At the suggestion of the king, Norman Hartnell is making her dresses in the romantic, graceful style of Franz Winterhalter's royal portraits. It is a winning combination, a queen who looks like a queen – with a smile.

A child may look at a Queen.

IRA bombers kill five in Coventry

Coventry, 25 August 1939
In the worst outrage since the IRA started its bombing campaign eight months ago, a bomb hidden in a tradesman's box-tricycle killed five people and injured 50 in Broadgate, Coventry's busy main street today. The bomb exploded just before 2.30, shattering shopfronts and blasting a large hole in the road. Cars were overturned, shards of glass sliced across the road. Handbags and children's toys lay among the debris. The centre of the city, which had been crowded with weekend shoppers, looked like a battlefield.

The bomb was not aimed at any military target but was designed to maim and kill ordinary people. Workmen said they had seen a young man run away from the scene of the explosion towards the railway station. He had already left on a Birmingham train before the police arrived. The bomb follows drastic new laws, including arrest without warrant, rushed through Parliament last month to curb the terrorists.

Hitler threatens Poland, and fear of war grows

London, 31 August 1939

The Polish crisis deepens by the hour; with his eastern front protected by his non-aggression pact with Stalin, Hitler is turning the screw on the Poles. They must either surrender Danzig and the Polish Corridor or face invasion from the massive German army gathered on their border. In fact, it seems that Hitler actually wants war but is delaying only in the hope that he can dissuade Britain and France from going to Poland's assistance. There is little chance of that. Both countries are committed by treaty to fight if Poland is invaded and Britain would not stomach another Munich.

Throughout Europe the nations are preparing for the inevitable conflict. Poland has ordered all reservists to the colours. France has also been calling up reservists and today all the railways were requisitioned. Belgium has announced that its frontiers and anti-aircraft defences are fully manned. Even Switzerland has mobilised. And the Red Army is gathering menacingly on Poland's eastern border.

In Britain, preparations for war can be seen everywhere. Trenches are being dug in London's parks. Sandbags mask the entrances to public buildings. Air raid shelters are being hastily completed. The evacuation of children began yesterday. Labelled, with a few possessions in a single home-made haversack and with gas masks round their necks, over 1.5 million are being taken from target areas to the safety of the countryside. The capital's

As war looms, the King, Queen and princesses join in community singing at the King's camp for boys near Balmoral.

moveable treasures, including the Coronation Chair, have also been evacuated. The Royal Navy has been mobilised and merchant ships requisitioned. Army and RAF reserves have been called up. The anti-aircraft forces have been deployed and key parties for coastal defence assembled. The government has sent warning telegrams to the dominion governments and the colonies.

The king, who was taking his summer holiday with his family at Balmoral when news of the Hitler-Stalin pact broke, drove to Perth where he boarded a special coach attached to the night express. Since then he has been hard at work, inspecting the newly-mobilised Auxiliary Fleet and visiting the War Office, the Admiralty, the Air Ministry and the Central War Room.

He also sought permission from Mr Chamberlain to make a personal approach to Hitler but Chamberlain said the time was "not opportune". The queen, having settled her daughters in the care of "Crawfie" at Birkhall on the Balmoral estate, hurried south to join her husband. She has no intention of leaving him to face alone the daunting task of leading the nation into war.

A miner and his pit pony make royal friends at Windsor Great Park show.

Princess Margaret celebrates her ninth birthday with her parents at Balmoral. ▷

War declared! Britain and France join

First air raid sirens sound over London

Ultimatum rejected: war official.

London, 3 September 1939

At 11.15 this morning Prime Minister Chamberlain told an anxious nation that no reply had been received to Britain's ultimatum to Hitler to cease his attack on Poland, "consequently this country is at war with Germany." Some hours later, the French ultimatum also ran out and the allies of 1914 found themselves once again united in war against oppression. Minutes after Chamberlain's broadcast the air raid sirens wailed and Londoners hurried to the shelters. It was a false alarm, but an indication of the destruction to come.

At six this evening, people gathered round their radio sets again, this time to listen to the king make a stirring call to arms: "We are called, with our allies, to meet the challenge of a principle which, if it were to prevail, would be fatal to any civilised order in the world ... the primitive doctrine that Might is Right ... It is unthinkable that we should refuse to meet the challenge ... To this high purpose I now call my people at home and my peoples across the seas. I ask them to stand firm and united in this time of trial."

His speech was clear and confident. It was as if the thought of action and duty had cleared his mind of all his self-doubt. He confides in his diary, "Today we are at war again ... the country is calm, firm and united behind its leaders, resolved to fight until Liberty and Justice are once again safe." The queen is at his side, insisting, "If things turn out badly, I must be with the king." But she no longer needs to put steel in his backbone. He has found his own courage.

Queen Elizabeth holds working parties in Buckingham Palace

London, 3 September 1939

The queen is determined to play a full part in the war. Even before the war started she had organised working parties of members and wives of the palace staff. Meeting, with tea and biscuits, round trestle tables set up in the palace's ornate Blue Drawing Room, they knit comforts for servicemen and make surgical dressings and clothes for the Red Cross. Their output may be small but the queen intends to show that the whole nation, from top to bottom, is involved in the war. Following her example working parties are being set up throughout the country. They are having an unintended social effect for the pictures of the queen sitting down to knit with her maids and the wives of her servants are helping to break down class barriers. It is a development which horrifies some of her courtiers but she, at least, understands that in order to win the war the old divisions must go. We are all in it together.

Members of the household staff of the palace and wives of employees meet to make clothes for the Red Cross.

forces as Hitler's war machine crushes Poland

Queen visits an evacuation school and chats with a boy digging for victory.

The Queen broadcasts to the mothers whose children have been evacuated.

An evacuee bathes her doll.

London, 11 November 1939

In an Armistice Day message broadcast from Buckingham Palace to the women of the empire today the queen said that in past conflicts women could do little more than encourage their men at the front. But all that has changed now: "we, no less than men, have real and vital work to do." Sympathising with women whose families have been split up by the war with their menfolk in the services and their children evacuated, the queen nevertheless reminded her listeners of their "proud privilege of serving our country in her hour of need".

She is setting a splendid example. While her husband is visiting the troops and attending to the affairs of state, she is travelling the country in the royal train, visiting evacuated children and the "billeters" who have taken them under their wing and reassuring anxious mothers that their children were in good hands. She has visited military hospitals, air raid shelters, munitions factories, the training camps of the women's services, Civil Defence depots and the barrage balloon units which ring the big cities. Just occasionally, she and the king take an evening off and, to make sure the people know they are still on duty in the capital, they go to the theatre where they are invariably greeted with cheers.

She seems to thrive on this punishing routine. Always beautifully turned-out, even in the grimiest of factories, she brings a glow to every place she visits. Chatting to the workers, showing an interest in what they do, flashing that famous smile, she is a great morale-booster and production always soars when she has toured a factory. In the midst of all this work the problem of the Duke of Windsor has returned to haunt the king and queen. The duke wants to return to England and be given a major wartime job with an important post for his wife. The king has refused and has asked his brother to serve with the Military Mission in Paris. To everyone's relief, the duke has accepted.

Feeling the texture: Queen visits barrage balloon station guarding London.

The royal family take an evening off from the war to visit the theatre.

1 Dec 1939. Mass deportation of Jews from German-occupied territories begins under the direction of Adolf Eichmann.

4 Dec 1939. King George visits the British army in France.

6 Dec 1939. Britain agrees to send arms to Finland.

12 Dec 1939. Actor Douglas Fairbanks dies aged 56.

17 Dec 1939. The German pocket battleship *Graf Spee* is scuttled in the River Plate after a fierce battle with British cruisers.

31 Dec 1939. Song-hit of the year: "We'll hang out the washing on the Siegfried Line."

3 Jan 1940. Unity Mitford, daughter of Lord Redesdale and friend of Hitler, comes home from Germany on a stretcher after attempting suicide.

17 Jan 1940. The Thames freezes for the first time since 1888 as Europe is gripped by icy weather.

29 Jan 1940. Laurence Olivier's wife, Jill Esmond, is granted a divorce.

11 Feb 1940. John Buchan, Lord Tweedsmuir, dies. He was the author of *The Thirty Nine Steps* and Governor General of Canada.

17 Feb 1940. Sailors from HMS *Cossack* rescue 300 British prisoners from the German ship *Altmark*.

1 March 1940. Vivien Leigh wins an Oscar for her portrayal of Scarlett O'Hara in *Gone With the Wind*.

7 March 1940. The liner *Queen Elizabeth* completes her secret maiden voyage to New York.

13 March 1940. The Russians finally defeat the Finns, but only at humiliating cost.

27 March 1940. Himmler orders the construction of a concentration camp at Auschwitz.

2 April 1940. Chamberlain tells Parliament: "Hitler has missed the bus."

9 April 1940. Hitler invades Denmark and Norway.

6 May 1940. John Steinbeck wins a Pulitzer Prize for his novel *The Grapes of Wrath*.

10 May 1940. Holland and Belgium fall to the German blitzkrieg.

31 May 1940. Sir Oswald Mosley, leader of the British Union of Fascists, is interned under Regulation 18B.

King swears to remain in uniform

The King, who fought at Jutland, wears his uniform with pride; the Queen, always feminine, remains in 'civvies'.

Sandringham, 25 December 1939
The king used his traditional Christmas Day broadcast today to rally the nation to the war effort. The allied cause, he said, was no less than the survival of "Christian civilisation". Although no one could see him, he made the broadcast wearing his uniform as admiral of the fleet for he has sworn to remain in uniform until the war has ended. The queen, on the other hand, has made up her mind not to wear uniform. She feels that they do not become her and, apart from rare appearances in Girl Guide uniform, always wears extremely feminine outfits and distinctive hats. She reasons: "When the people come to see me they put on their best clothes; I shall do the same for them."

Phoney war is broken by a sea battle in the South Atlantic

London, 23 February 1940
With the armies of both sides sitting looking at each other in France in the so-called "phoney" war, it has taken an heroic sea battle to stir the imagination of the country. On December 13th, the cruisers *Exeter*, *Ajax* and the *Achilles* of the New Zealand navy fought the pocket battleship *Graf Spee* off the River Plate estuary. In the battle the lighter *Exeter* and *Ajax* suffered heavy damage but the *Graf Spee* was also hit, and after taking refuge in Montevideo, she was scuttled by her captain, Hans Langsdorff, who then committed suicide. When the *Exeter* finally reached Plymouth eight days ago she was welcomed by Winston Churchill, First Lord of the Admiralty. Today, the king and queen met the widows and children of the men who died on *Ajax* and *Exeter*. The king, who had fought at Jutland, moved among the grieving families with his wife. They offered their condolences in the certain knowledge that many more men would die and many more families would grieve.

Churchill under HMS 'Exeter's guns.

The King and Queen meet the families of the crews of 'Ajax' and 'Exeter'.

Blitzkrieg in the West: Hitler strikes at France

Paris, 16 May 1940

The allies are reeling under the hammer blows of Hitler's panzers. Denmark has been occupied; Norway has fallen. The Belgian and Dutch armies have been swept aside and there is panic in Paris as the French and British troops fall back in confusion. Ministries are burning their confidential documents and Prime Minister Paul Renaud, pleading with Winston Churchill to send more fighter squadrons to France, has told the newly appointed British premier that "the road to Paris is open" and that "the battle is lost."

Churchill arrived here this afternoon to assess the situation for himself and to bolster French morale. He is appalled by French official defeatism which is all-pervasive despite the gallant efforts by a tank commander, Colonel Charles de Gaulle, to stop the Germans. Realising the gravity of the situation, Churchill has asked the Cabinet to approve the sending of more fighters to France despite Britain's own danger. "It would not be good his-

Princess Juliana of Holland and her family are refugees in London.

A smile for Dunkirk wounded.

torically", he telegraphed the Cabinet, "if the French requests were denied and their ruin resulted."

In another telegram he has told President Roosevelt: "The small countries are simply smashed up, one by one, like matchwood." Britain also expects to be attacked, he said, "both from the air and by parachute and air-borne troops in the near future, and are getting ready for them." The devastation in Europe has reached into Buckingham Palace where the king and queen are "billeters" for royal refugees. Princess Juliana of Holland has arrived with her young family with only what they are wearing. King Haakon and Crown Prince Olav of Norway have also taken shelter in the palace. The king and queen are making their own preparations for the German onslaught. They will stay and fight.

Rationing imposed as war bites

London, April 1940

Rationing, brought about by the shortage of shipping capacity, was imposed on the nation today for the first time since 1918. Butter, sugar, bacon and ham can only be bought on production of ration books. Everyone will get the same four ounces of butter a week, 12 ounces of sugar, four ounces of uncooked bacon or ham, and three and a half ounces of cooked bacon or ham. Coupons will not be needed in restaurants or canteens but hotel guests are required to hand over their ration books. Meat rationing will be introduced next month on the basis of value rather than weight. Offal, rabbits, poultry, game and fish will not require coupons for the time being, nor will brawn, sausages, pies or pâté. The Ministry of Food believes that the scheme, which entails the registration of every household with local shops, will distribute supplies more efficiently. It should also ensure a healthier diet for the poorer sections of the community.

Chamberlain is sacked: Churchill, the old warrior, takes over

Mr and Mrs Winston Churchill enter No 10 Downing Street to take up office.

London, 10 May 1940

King George reluctantly accepted Neville Chamberlain's resignation as Prime Minister today in the face of battlefield disasters. The king and queen are sad to see him go. They looked on him as a friend and a wise leader who bought time for the country with the Munich agreement. They approved of his policy of appeasement for, like so many of their subjects, they remembered the Great War with horror. They have both written to thank him for his support "during these last desperate and unhappy years".

Given that he had to go, they would have preferred Lord Halifax, another appeaser, as his successor. Instead they have been forced to accept Winston Churchill to whom they are bitterly opposed because they think he is an unreliable political adventurer and, more personally, because he supported the Duke of Windsor during the abdication crisis. But parliament is determined to have a fighting leader. The old warrior Churchill is its choice and the king must comply.

▷

17 June 1940. Liner *Lancastria* sunk while evacuating soldiers and refugees: 2,800 die.

9 July 1940. Duke of Windsor is appointed Governor of the Bahamas.

23 July 1940. Government imposes 24 per cent tax on luxury goods.

20 August 1940. Churchill praises RAF: "Never in the field of human conflict was so much owed by so many to so few."

21 August 1940. Exiled Bolshevik leader, Leon Trotsky, assassinated in Mexico City by a Stalin agent wielding an ice-pick.

24 Sept 1940. King introduces the George Cross and George Medal "For valour and outstanding gallantry."

21 Oct 1940. Ernest Hemingway publishes *For Whom the Bell Tolls.*

5 Nov 1940. Roosevelt is elected for record third term as president.

9 Nov 1940. Neville Chamberlain, haunted by Munich, dies. He was 71.

5 Jan 1941. Amy Johnson, renowned woman pilot, drowns after ditching in Thames.

12 Feb 1941. Policeman with septicaemia is cured by new drug, penicillin.

28 March 1941. Virgina Woolf, novelist and "Bloomsbury" literary figure, drowns herself.

10 May 1941. Hitler's deputy, Rudolf Hess, lands in Scotland on "peace mission".

24 May 1941. HMS *Hood* is sunk by the *Bismarck*. More than 1,400 men die. *Bismarck* is sunk three days later.

4 June 1941. Former Kaiser Wilhelm II dies in Holland.

14 August 1941. Churchill and Roosevelt proclaim Atlantic Charter after meeting at sea.

8 July 1942. British-born actor Cary Grant marries Woolworth heiress Barbara Hutton.

19 August 1942. Allied raid on Dieppe is repulsed with heavy casualties.

30 Oct 1942. General Montgomery defeats Rommel at El Alamein.

26 Nov 1942. Russian offensive traps German 6th Army in Stalingrad.

1 Dec 1942. The Beveridge Report, Britain's blueprint for postwar social security, is unveiled.

British army is rescued from Dunkirk

The 'little boats' bring the men home

Dover, 4 June 1940
The "Miracle of Dunkirk" is over. The battered British army has been lifted from the shell-swept beaches along with thousands of French and Belgian troops by an armada of little ships and carried to safety across the Channel in "Operation Dynamo". The last of the men rescued from annihilation were being landed tonight from destroyers, ferries, trawlers, paddle steamers, even weekend motor boats. Welcomed with mugs of tea and waving Union Jacks, they are being put on trains to depots where they will be retrained and re-equipped to fight again.

However, although the nation is regarding Dunkirk as more of a victory than a defeat, there can be no doubting the seriousness of the situation. Most of the army's heavy equipment has been lost. The RAF and the Royal Navy have sustained serious losses and, unless France can be persuaded to fight on, there will be little to stop the Germans if they cross the Channel. Curiously, faced with this danger, the nation's morale is sky-high.

Weary British soldiers struggle to reach the rescuers off Dunkirk beach.

France falls to German blitzkrieg

Paris, 16 June 1940
Paris has fallen, the government has fled, the Swastika flies over the Eiffel Tower and France's resistance has crumbled in the face of the relentless German onslaught. In a last desperate effort to sustain the battle, Churchill had proposed that Britain and France should no longer be two nations but a single Franco-British Union with common citizenship to resist "a system which reduces mankind to a life of robots and slaves". There has been no reply, the government and the people are demoralised and there is little doubt that Britain will soon stand alone against Germany. Churchill is looking elsewhere for help. He has appealed to America to "bring her powerful material aid to the common cause. And thus we shall conquer".

Queen Elizabeth will not be leaving

London, 20 June 1940
With the German army looking across the Channel, many upper-class British families are sending their children to safety in North America, but when it was suggested to the queen that the two princesses should be sent to Canada, she was indignant: "The children will not go without me, I won't leave without the king, and the king would never leave." The royal family is guarded by a special unit ordered to get them to safety if German paratroops land, but the king and queen are preparing to defend themselves, practising every day on firing ranges in the grounds of Buckingham Palace and Windsor Castle. The queen has a favourite revolver given to her by Winston Churchill. "I shall not go down like the others," she says.

Battle rages in Britain's skies

London 20 August 1940
Prime Minister Churchill paid tribute tonight to the RAF pilots who are fighting the Battle of Britain. "Never in the field of human conflict", he declared, "was so much owed by so many to so few." The young pilots, heavily outnumbered, tear into the Germans who must clear the RAF from the skies before they can launch their invasion. Never before has the Luftwaffe encountered such resistance. The "Few" symbolise the spirit of resistance which now prevails in Britain. The king and queen are determined to fight to the end. On receiving a letter from King Gustav of Sweden offering his services as an intermediary with Hitler "to examine the possibilities of peace", the king rejected the proposal out of hand.

The Luftwaffe rains destruction on Britain's cities

Inspecting the damage after Buckingham Palace is hit by German bomber.

The royal couple tour the blitzed East End of London after a raid.

Take cover! In the shelter.

Dinner for the bombed-out.

London, 13 September 1940

A lone German bomber flew low up the Mall this morning and, taking deliberate aim, dropped its bombs on Buckingham Palace. The king and queen, who were in their sitting room, actually saw the bombs falling, were showered with splintered glass and narrowly escaped death. Afterwards, inspecting the wrecked chapel, the queen said, "I'm almost glad we've been bombed. Now I can look the East End in the face." The royal couple visited the smoking ruins of the blitzed areas almost every day, comforting the bombed-out people, taking shelter with them when the sirens sounded. The East-enders, at first resentful that they seemed to be taking all the punishment, adored "Queenie". Typical of them was the woman who watched the queen help a mother with a disabled arm dress her baby. "Oh, ain't she lovely", said the cockney, "ain't she just bloody lovely." As the Luftwaffe spreads its attacks outside London, so the king and queen spend many hours travelling by train to inspect the damage and bring comfort to the victims, often sleeping in lonely sidings, protected by the Home Guard. They are completely immersed in their war work, boosting morale wherever they go. So great is the queen's impact an American newspaper has named her the "Minister for Morale".

Heroes of the blitz: the Queen touring raided areas talks to ARP workers.

Chatting to an armaments worker in a factory 'somewhere in the North'.

73

Germany attacks the Soviet Union

Moscow, 22 June 1941

At 4.15 this morning German tanks crashed across the border into the Soviet Union while the Luftwaffe bombed 66 Soviet airfields in an attempt to win another blitzkrieg victory. The invasion has taken Moscow by surprise, with Stalin unable to believe that his ally, Hitler, could betray him. The Germans have massed 100 divisions and with their Finnish and Rumanian allies are invading from the Arctic Circle to the Black Sea, brushing aside the unprepared Red Army. Churchill, who has no love for the Bolsheviks but hates the Nazis more, has reacted by promising the Russians "whatever help we can; we have offered any technical or economic assistance in our power". He went on: "We are resolved to destroy Hitler and every vestige of the Nazi regime. From this nothing will turn us. We will never parley, never."

Japan strikes at Pearl Harbour

Pearl Harbour, 7 December 1941

The United States is at war following a sneak attack early this morning by Japanese carrier-borne aircraft on the US Pacific Fleet at Pearl Harbour in Hawaii. The attack, on a quiet Sunday morning, caught the US Navy completely unawares and in two hours the Japanese planes sank or seriously damaged five battleships and 14 smaller ships, destroyed 200 aircraft and killed more than 2,400 people. Other attacks were mounted against American bases in the Philippines and on Guam and Wake islands in the central Pacific. There are reports of Japanese invasion forces moving against British, Dutch and French possessions. The whole of the Pacific is ablaze. The only consolation for the Americans as they view the destruction of their fleet is that their all-important aircraft carriers were not in Pearl Harbour and escaped the carnage. President Roosevelt describes today as "a day of infamy" but Churchill, while sympathising with the Americans, now knows that Britain, so long alone, cannot lose the war.

Princess Elizabeth is sixteen and officially enters public life

Windsor, 25 April 1942

It is Princess Elizabeth's sixteenth birthday today and she marked her entry into public life by taking the salute at a march past of the Grenadier Guards. It was something of a family affair; she has been made Colonel of the regiment and knows most of the young officers who are invited to tea at the castle and provide the young princesses with a hint of the exciting, unknown male world outside the court. She wants to see more of that world and, following her parents' example, is anxious to "do her bit" for the war effort. Like all other sixteen-year-old girls she is now required to register at the local labour exchange for war service. Technically, once she has registered she will be liable to be called up to serve in a munitions factory, or as a nurse or in the women's forces. The princess, who has told her father, "I ought to do as other girls of my age do", would like to be a nurse or join the ATS. The queen, remembering

Happy birthday: Princess Elizabeth takes salute from the Grenadier Guards.

her own experience of comforting the wounded at Glamis in the last war, is sympathetic but she will not argue with the king about it and he will not hear of it. He thinks his daughter is far too young and, un- like his wife, cannot come to terms with the idea that his Lilibet should want to become involved with the wartime world outside the palace. So Elizabeth, who will one day be Queen of England, must wait.

The Duke of Kent is killed in an aircrash while flying to Iceland

Invergordon, 25 August 1942

The Duke of Kent was killed today when the Sunderland flying boat, in which he was flying to Iceland to inspect RAF bases, crashed into a hill on the Duke of Portland's estate. The 39-year-old duke died instantly. The king and queen, on holiday at Balmoral, learnt of his death while they were dining with the Duke and Duchess of Gloucester. Greatly dis- tressed, they all left for London tonight. The duke's death is par- ticularly poignant because he had emerged from a notorious period of his life into a happy marriage to Princess Marina which produced three children – Edward, Alexandra and Michael, who was christened just three weeks ago. Marina, told of her husband's death by her chil- dren's nanny, is distraught. Having gone to bed early she sensed there was something wrong as she heard the nanny's footsteps approaching and cried out, "It's George, isn't it?" The death of the duke, the youngest and most cultured of the royal brothers, and once thought to be better kingly material than his older brother, has brought home to the country the fact that in this war everybody is at risk.

Duke of Kent chats to Polish flier.

RAF provide a guard of honour for the Duke's body on its way to Windsor.

Mrs Roosevelt samples wartime rations

A meagre lunch at Claridge's.

London, November 1942
Eleanor Roosevelt, who has arrived in England to visit American troops on behalf of her husband, has seen for herself how wartime hardships are affecting everybody in Britain. At Buckingham Palace she was given a bedroom with boarded up windows, lit by a solitary bulb and heated by one bar of an electric radiator. At dinner she was served a sparse meal of ordinary rations – but on a golden plate. The king insists on being treated like everyone else. In order to save on heating he has had lines painted round the baths. Nobody is allowed more than five inches of water, unless it is cold.

Mother and daughters pose before the mock orange at Windsor Castle.

The royal family has posed for a series of official but charming pictures at Windsor Castle and Buckingham Palace, showing the queen in the role of teacher to her daughters in the garden at Windsor and with the king at the palace which was much battered by German bombs in last year's raids.

Canada's soldiers come to help Britain

The Queen inspects tough troops of the newly arrived Canadian division.

London, Autumn 1942
The queen, who has a special affection for the Canadians who welcomed her so warmly on her pre-war tour, has been visiting the soldiers who have come to help the mother-country at their bases "somewhere in England". These fine fighting men are eager to get to grips with the enemy. They want revenge for the reverse they suffered in the Dieppe raid in August. Thousands of them are crossing the Atlantic and, while the Australians, New Zealanders and Indians are pre-occupied in the Middle East and Far East, the Canadians will form the third major contingent with the British and the Americans when the time comes to liberate Europe.

Queen's family home becomes a hospital

Hertfordshire, Autumn 1942
The queen has paid a visit to St Paul's Walden Bury, her family's English country house, which has been turned into a convalescent home for servicemen recovering from their wounds. She led the way through well-remembered rooms, chatted to the soldiers as she had learnt to do at Glamis in the last war, joined the young men round the billiards table and then sat in an armchair outside what had been her own backdoor to have her picture taken with the patients and their nurses. It was all a far cry from the day when she accepted Bertie's proposal in the nearby garden.

Romantic memories: the Queen returns to the house where 'Bertie' proposed. ▷

King goes to war, visits Desert Rats

North Africa, 20 June 1943

The king visited the battered George Cross island of Malta today, just sixty miles from enemy airfields on Sicily. He is in the middle of a gruelling tour of the Middle East, reviewing the allied armies preparing to assault Italy. He has travelled as "General Lyon", flying from England in Churchill's converted Lancaster bomber. In Tunisia he was quickly recognised by the renowned Desert Rats and was cheered by the men as he walked among them in the scorching midsummer heat.

He has also visited the American troops in Algiers and Harold MacMillan, newly appointed Minister Resident to the allied forces, reports: "The Americans were really delighted and letters about it will reach every distant part of the USA." He has had discussions with General Montgomery and the US commander, General Eisenhower, and, in the interests of diplomacy, lunched between two rival French leaders, General de Gaulle and General Giraud.

His punishing schedule, the heat, the flies and a bad attack of stomach trouble have begun to tell on him and he has had a couple of bouts of his famous "gnashes" when nobody is safe from his temper. Without the queen to calm him even the generals are suffering, but today he is relaxed, happy to be in Malta.

The King lunches in the field with US General Patton and his staff.

The King's 'battle wagon' passes line of Sherman tanks in North Africa.

Queen fights on the Home Front while King tours Middle East

London, 20 June 1943

The queen, like so many other wives, is worrying and waiting while her husband is in the war zone. She has told Queen Mary of her fears when the king's plane was diverted because of fog: "I imagined every sort of horror." He appointed her a Counsellor of State before he left and she is carrying out his many duties, including holding an investiture at which she decorated the Dambuster hero Guy Gibson with the Victoria Cross. She has also been overseeing the farm which was established on 1,500 acres of Windsor Great Park, ploughed up and planted with cereals as part of the vital "Dig for Victory" campaign to counter Hitler's effort to starve Britain with his U-boat blockade.

The Queen and her farm manager examine the barley crop at Sandringham.

Third birthday for American volunteers

The Queen inspects American Ambulance drivers at Buckingham Palace.

London, 22 June 1943
Members of the American Ambulance Service paraded at Buckingham Palace today to be inspected by the queen in celebration of their third anniversary. The service, financed by Americans and manned by American volunteers, was formed in the dangerous days of the Blitz and has done marvellous work. It is just one example of private US aid to Britain ranging from "Bundles for Britain" to the team of pilots who formed the "Eagle Squadron", and much of this aid can be traced directly to the winning of American hearts and minds by the king and queen with their 1939 tour.

A royal visit for US Army bomber base

East Anglia, 17 August 1943
Today the king and queen visited a USAAF base "somewhere in England" to pay their respects to the bomber crews who are flying their Liberators and Flying Fortresses on daily raids, carrying the war into the heart of Germany. East Anglia is studded with airfields from which the bombers take off to build huge formations before setting course across the North Sea on the shortest route to their targets. These airfields are like small pieces of America set down in England and the visit of the king and queen was something quite outside the experience of the American fliers.

American soldiers come to attention for the royals at their English base.

RAF's 'bomber boys' welcome royal family

Enjoying a joke with RAF bomber crews at their East Anglian airfield.

East Anglia, Autumn 1943
This is something for the boys to write home about. The young men who, in their own words, "dice with death" in the dangerous night skies over Germany, gave a tremendous welcome to the royal family when they visited a bomber base in East Anglia. Formal discipline vanished when the royals went "walk-about" among the pilots, air gunners and navigators, most of them not much older than Princess Elizabeth. The king, who learnt to fly in 1919 in a tiny Avro 504k, was fascinated by its huge successors, the Avro Lancasters, flown with such skill and dedication by the laughing youngsters.

The Queen's father dies at Glamis Castle

Glamis, 7 November 1944
The queen's father, the Earl of Strathmore, died here today at the age of 89. He is to be buried in a private ceremony alongside his wife in the grounds of the castle. The queen, who is much distressed by his death, will attend the funeral. Claude Bowes Lyon, despite his many titles, his land and considerable wealth, was essentially a family man who instilled in his children a sense of duty and a love of the countryside. He was never happier than walking the hills around Glamis. It is this background allied to the sense of fun inherited from her mother that sustains the queen.

The Earl of Strathmore: a beloved father dies at 89 after a life of service.

20 Jan 1945. President Roosevelt is inaugurated for his record fourth term of office.

12 Feb 1945. Churchill, Stalin and Roosevelt settle the form of the post-war world at Yalta.

14 Feb 1945. RAF and USAAF bombers reduce Dresden to a pile of smoking ruins.

26 March 1945. Earl Lloyd George, spellbinding Welsh orator, dies at 82.

12 April 1945. Franklin Roosevelt dies suddenly at 63. He is succeeded by Vice President Harry Truman.

30 April 1945. Belsen, Dachau and Buchenwald are liberated. Churchill says of concentration camps: "No words can express our horror."

29 May 1945. William Joyce, better known as "Lord Haw Haw", is arrested.

21 June 1945. The Battle for Okinawa ends in victory for the Americans after 83 days of bloody fighting.

26 July 1945. The nation rejects Winston Churchill in first post-war general election. Labour, under Clement Attlee, win in a landslide.

6 August 1945. Hiroshima is vaporised by an atomic bomb: 70,000 die.

30 Jan 1946. King George makes speech of welcome at the inaugural session of the United Nations in London.

27 Feb 1946. *Road to Utopia* starring Bob Hope, Bing Crosby and Dorothy Lamour opens in New York.

5 March 1946. Churchill warns that an "Iron Curtain" has descended across the Continent."

1 May 1946. Scientist Alan Nunn May is jailed for 10 years for passing nuclear secrets to the USSR.

30 May 1946. Bread is rationed for the first time as austerity Britain tightens its belt.

5 June 1946. The Derby, run at Epsom for first time in six years, is won by *Airborne*.

22 July 1946. Time-bomb planted by Jewish terrorists destroys British HQ in King David Hotel, Jerusalem, with heavy casualties.

16 Oct 1946. Ten top Nazis are executed at Nuremberg. Goering cheats the hangman by taking poison.

22 Nov 1946. The Biro, a pen which writes 200,000 words without refilling, goes on sale.

Princess Elizabeth goes to war: she joins the ATS as officer cadet

Camberley, Surrey, March 1945

Princess Elizabeth, who is 19 next month, has at last overcome her father's objections and has been allowed to play a part in the war. She is now No 230873 Second Subaltern Elizabeth Windsor of the Auxiliary Transport Service and spends her days delving into the oily insides of army lorries. She still sleeps at Windsor but otherwise is just one of the girls. She is learning how to maintain vehicles, read a map and drive in convoy; her first reports describe her as "efficient, quick and neat". She has had some shocks, however. She was appalled at the preparation that went into a visit to her unit by her aunt, the Princess Royal. She wrote to her former nannie, Crawfie: "Spit and polishing the whole day long. Now I realise what must happen when Papa and Mama go anywhere. That's something I shall never forget."

The new recruit explains to her mother what she has learnt about car engines.

Hitler and Mussolini die violently in the ruins of their empires

Berlin, 30 April 1945

Hitler committed suicide in the ruins of his Chancellery today just two days after Mussolini, his partner in evil, was shot by partisans and strung up by his heels from the facade of a garage in Milan's Piazza Loretto. The squalid deaths of these two men who thought they could rule the world mark the closing stages of the war in Europe. Italy has fallen and the Allies are swarming through the rubble of the Reich that was to "last a thousand years".

Nowhere will the end of hostilities be greeted with more relief than in Buckingham Palace – damaged on no less than nine occasions by bombs and V1s. The king, still mourning for his brother, the Duke of Kent, has grown weary and more tetchy as the war has dragged on. His tiredness is etched in his face and he admits: "I'm whacked." He has hardly had a day off duty in more than five years. He has undertaken gruelling inspections of the forces in the Middle East and in France soon after D-Day. He, along with the queen, has covered more than 50,000 miles by train, visiting bombed cities and boosting morale throughout the country. They have proved themselves true leaders of their people in times of utmost dan-

ger and the royal family has never been so popular. But, never strong, he has paid a heavy price and the queen fears for his health.

She, on the other hand, has thrived on her punishing schedule. She never seems to weary and when asked how she can smile all the time, she replies: "I don't know how not to smile." There is nothing false about it. Her concern shines through and when she appeared among the bombed-out cockneys during the Blitz they knew immedi-

ately she was "a good'un". However, what has not been recognised outside court circles is that apart from her public work she has also borne a tremendous private burden, sustaining the king and calming him when one of his "gnashes" threatens. It is indeed doubtful if he, for all his undoubted courage, could have survived the war without her. It is with justice that Winston Churchill, once regarded by her as an enemy but now a firm friend, refers to her as "that valiant woman".

American and Russian soldiers meet amidst the devastation of Berlin.

City goes wild as huge crowds celebrate VE Day

London, 8 May 1945

The whole of London along with thousands of Allied troops took to the streets today to celebrate victory. They headed for Buckingham Palace, battered and with its windows boarded but still the centre of national feeling. There was a huge roar as Churchill drove through the gates on his way to lunch with the king and queen. Then, at 3 pm the vast congregation fell silent, listening to the prime minister broadcast over loudspeakers. Although Japan remained to be conquered, he said, the war in Europe would end at midnight. "Advance Britannia!" he proclaimed. "Long live the cause of freedom! God Save the King!"

It was the signal for the release of years of pent-up feelings. The dancing, singing crowd surged round the palace gates demanding, "We want the king!" The royal family stepped into the sunlight on the balcony, the king, queen and princesses, holding hands. It was the first of eight such appearances. Churchill joined them and then when it grew dark the

Peace at last: the royal family and Winston Churchill greet the happy crowds from Buckingham Palace balcony.

princesses, accompanied by Guards officers, slipped out to mingle in the crowd, shouting, "We want the king!" They then sent back a message to their parents: "Come out, we want to see what it's like from this side", and the king and queen duly obliged. Back in Whitehall, the prime minister, dressed in his famous siren suit, conducted the crowd in singing "Land of Hope and Glory". Tomorrow the king and queen are driving to the East End to celebrate with their friends of the Blitz.

Liberated Channel Islands welcome royals

Channel Islands, 7 June 1945

The king and queen dashed here today on board the cruiser HMS *Jamaica* to visit the only British territory to be occupied by the Nazis. On Guernsey, thousands turned out to celebrate their liberation and greet the royal couple as they walked through the Candle Gardens. On Jersey the islanders waved festoons of red, white and blue bunting as the king and queen walked in procession to the States, the island parliament. While the islands were occupied, they were subject to the same regime as the rest of Europe with all its attendant horrors. "After long suffering", the king told the States, "I hope the island will soon regain its former glory."

Atom bomb forces Japan to surrender

Tokyo, 15 August 1945

Japan has surrendered unconditionally. At midday today Emperor Hirohito broadcast to his people for the first time to tell them that they have lost the war. Many Japanese want to continue the struggle despite the crushing defeats they have suffered, but the destruction of Hiroshima and Nagasaki by atomic bombs has convinced the emperor that it is useless to fight on against these awesome weapons. The news has been greeted with relief by allied forces preparing to invade Japan against fanatical opposition. The bombs have saved the lives of hundreds of thousands of allied soldiers.

So ends the war, which for Britain has lasted only a few days short of six years. The return of peace is to be celebrated by two days of public holiday and a broadcast by the king. The new prime minister, Clement Attlee, spoke to the nation by radio at midnight, declaring: "Japan has today surrendered. The last of our enemies is laid low."

Agricultural experts visit royal farms

Windsor, August 1945

The queen is acting as host to a conference of agricultural experts studying the modern methods employed on the royal farms. Established on parkland ploughed up for wartime food, they are leading a revolution in British agriculture.

The queen chats to islanders freed after five years of German occupation.

The farmer's wife dressed for rain.

1947

The royals set out for holiday and political tour of South Africa

Cape Town, 21 April 1947

Princess Elizabeth celebrated her 21st birthday today by making a broadcast over South African Radio in which she dedicated herself to the service of the Commonwealth. It was well received, but this long tour by the royal family is not proving a success. Designed to give the king a rest after his wartime exertions, to support General Smuts in the South African elections and to provide the princess with time to consider her determination to marry Prince Philip, the tour is failing in all its aims.

An exhausting programme in intense heat is making the king bad tempered. He feels his place is back in a Britain suffering under one of the harshest winters on record. The South Africans are being insensitive and the royal party is encountering hostility from Smuts' Boer opponents and, as far as Princess Elizabeth is concerned, absence is making her heart grow fonder.

All this is causing tension in the royal party, and a few days ago the queen exploded when a man ran up to the royal car. Thinking he was an assassin, she beat him over the head with her parasol when all he was trying to do was give the princess a 10 shilling note as a birthday present. She dropped the broken parasol and continued waving to the crowd but was mortified when she learnt the truth.

Happy family on their way to the African sunshine after five years of war.

Posing on top of Table Mountain with the old warrior General Smuts.

Fighter ace Peter Townsend accompanies royal family to Africa

Peter Townsend, pilot and courtier.

Cape Town, 21 April 1947

One figure stands out among the 10 courtiers accompanying the royal family on their tour of South Africa. He is the elegant, handsome Battle of Britain fighter ace Group Captain Peter Townsend who arrived at Buckingham Palace three years ago when he was 30 on a three-month appointment as equerry to the king. Shy and sensitive, he fitted in immediately, and a father-son relationship has grown between the pilot and the king. His appointment has been indefinitely extended and as a mark of affection the king became godfather to Hugo George, second son of Townsend and his wife Rosemary in February 1945.

One of the reasons for his success is that he is able to cope with the king when he develops one of his fearsome "gnashes" and other courtiers take cover. This ability is appreciated by the queen and the princesses who also like to have a dashing RAF officer with them instead of the usual – and often boring – Guards officers. He accompanies them to the theatre, dances well and makes them laugh.

The constant demands of life at court have not helped his marriage. At first his wife was dazzled by being so close to the royal family but that has worn off and they are drifting apart. In these circumstances other courtiers have become somewhat anxious about the obvious affection shown him by the 16-year-old Princess Margaret. Some dismiss it as a case of puppy-love, other fear it may grow into something more serious.

It's official: Elizabeth is to wed Philip of Greece

Buckingham Palace, 10 July 1947
Princess Elizabeth has finally overcome her mother and father's misgivings about her love for Prince Philip. After months of rumour, the king officially announced today the engagement of "The Princess Elizabeth to Lieutenant Philip Mountbatten RN", adding that he had "gladly given his consent". That may be so but he still thinks that she is too young to marry and that she fell in love with the first eligible man she met. But he has been outgunned by his daughter's determination and by the manoeuvering of Philip's uncle, Lord Mountbatten, who has ambitions to get close to the throne.

The news was not in fact due to be made public for another five days but the secret leaked out and forced the premature announcement. During the waiting period a number of difficulties were overcome. The problem of Philip's Greek citizenship was easily solved. He filled in form "S", specially designed to grant British citizenship to foreign nationals who have fought for the United Kingdom. Philip, who had taken part in a number of sea battles in the Mediterranean and was Men-

Smiles all round for the engagement picture of Elizabeth and Philip.

tioned in Despatches, qualified with honour. The Greek royal family gave him permission to change his religion from Greek Orthodox to Church of England. Philip also acquired a surname; as a member of the Greek royal family he did not have one, but with the encouragement of his uncle he has become a Mountbatten.

The one problem that he has not as yet been able to overcome is his lack of funds. His family is notoriously impecunious and he has nothing but his Royal Navy lieutenant's pay of £11 a week to live on. No doubt some arrangement will be made but for the moment his financial embarrassment is so severe he has been unable to buy his fiancee an engagement ring. Curiously, it was because of this that news of the engagement leaked out. He approached his mother, Princess Andrew of Greece, who agreed to break down a tiara to make a ring and bracelet for Elizabeth. She gave the job to a London jeweller but two days ago, when she went to pick up the ring, someone tipped off the newspapers and, as a result, the announcement was hurried forward.

Britain's colonies demand their freedom

London, 15 August 1947
The British Empire "on which the sun never sets" is in retreat all round the world in the aftermath of the war. Britain no longer has the power or the will to hold on to its increasingly rebellious possessions and the king and queen find themselves rulers of a shrinking domain. The king's cousin, Lord Mountbatten, is presiding over the dissolution of the Indian Raj, the "jewel in the crown", and, following the passage of the India Independence Act a month ago, the king may no longer use the title of "Imperator" that was bestowed on Queen Victoria 70 years ago in recognition of Britain's Imperial rule over India.

Other colonial possessions – dominions, protectorates, dependencies – thought secure before the war, are demanding their freedom. Burma is moving towards independence and South Africa seems likely to fall to the Nationalists in the forthcoming election. Jews, seeking a new life

in the mandated territory of Palestine, are fighting a bitter civil war against the Arabs and the British army. There is talk of independence throughout the empire, from Africa to the Caribbean and the Pacific. So many former colonies seem set to gain their freedom that a ceremony has been devised for the occasion with the Union Jack being lowered at midnight as the flag of the new nation is unfurled.

In place of empire, the concept of the British Commonwealth of Nations is gaining ground. It is a curious, particularly British device. Its members, of whatever race, colour or type of government, with only their former subjugation by Britain uniting them, are equal under the figurehead of the king. He has no power, except that of example, and the members of the commonwealth may opt out whenever they wish. Like so many aspects of Britain's monarchy, it has evolved by accident but it seems to work.

A day at the races: The Queen and Princess Elizabeth walk the course at Epsom on Derby Day. They are both keen race-goers and love the Derby with its festive atmosphere of the Londoner on holiday.

Princess Elizabeth and Prince Philip

The royal bride and her husband are married by the Archbishop of Canterbury at the altar in Westminster Abbey.

London, 20 November 1947

Princess Elizabeth, the heir to the British throne, was married today to Lieutenant Philip Mountbatten, newly created Prince Philip, Duke of Edinburgh. Thousands of people, desperately in need of some splendour in the dreary austerity of post-war Britain, waited along the Mall and Whitehall. Many of them had slept out all night and they cheered wildly as the king and his daughter drove to Westminster Abbey in the Irish State coach escorted by the Household Cavalry, resplendent in their scarlet tunics. Like all other brides, the princess was granted an extra allotment of clothing coupons for her wedding dress, but hers was designed by Norman Hartnell and decorated with pearls and crystals.

Former Premier Baldwin dies

London, 14 December 1947

Lord Baldwin of Bewdley, who, as Prime Minister Stanley Baldwin, played a major role in bringing the king and queen to the throne, has died at the age of 80. An emollient pipe-smoking Tory, he was, nevertheless, prepared to risk everything to make sure that Edward VIII did not marry Wallis Simpson and remain on the throne. Although opposed by many at the time of the abdication, the nation has come to see that he was right. He has never been forgiven, however, for complacently neglecting Britain's defences in the face of the rise of Hitler and massive German rearmament.

For the family album: the official wedding picture in Buckingham Palace.

pledge their love in romantic Abbey ceremony

London, 20 November 1947

The government wanted the wedding of Princess Elizabeth and Prince Philip to be a low-key occasion in keeping with the harshness of the times, and the Archbishop of Canterbury stressed that the ceremony was as simple as for "any cottager who might be married in some small country church in the Dales this afternoon." But that was not what the people wanted; they wanted traditional glamour and they gathered at Buckingham Palace and cheered until the royal family appeared. A great roar went up when the bride and groom, flanked by the king and queen and the indomitable figure of the dowager Queen Mary, walked onto the balcony. The official photographs were taken in the palace and then the guests sat down to the wedding breakfast with a spray of lucky white heather, sent down from Balmoral, by every plate.

The speeches were kept mercifully short, and when the newlyweds drove out of the main courtyard in an open carriage they were showered with paper rose petals by their laughing guests who followed them to the gates, where the crowd greeted them as they drove – suitably warmed by hot-water bottles under their travelling rugs – to catch the royal train to Broadlands, the Hampshire home of "Uncle Dickie" Mountbatten, where they will start their honeymoon.

They will live at Clarence House for which Parliament has just voted £50,000 for refurbishment. There is no doubt that her parents will miss her, just like the parents of any other 21-year-old girl, but although she loves them dearly, she is anxious to get away from the palace. She wants to taste the world outside, to lead the life of a wife of a serving naval officer before, inevitably, she has to take up the more onerous duties of ruling the nation.

Elizabeth and Philip leave the abbey after the wedding ceremony.

The happy bride and groom in traditional pose after the ceremony.

The royal family appear on the Buckingham Palace balcony to salute the cheering crowd celebrating the wedding.

The newly-weds on their honeymoon walk through the grounds of Lord Mounbatten's estate at Romsey.

30 Jan 1948. India's saintly leader, Mahatma Gandhi, is assassinated by a fanatical Hindu, Nathuram Godse.

11 Feb 1948. Sergei Eisenstein, Soviet film director who made *The Battleship Potemkin*, dies of heart attack.

27 Feb 1948. Communists seize power in Czechoslovakia.

10 March 1948. Czech statesman Jan Masaryk falls, or was pushed, from a window in Prague. He was 61.

1 April 1948. Soviet Union clamps blockade on Berlin.

14 May 1948. The new state of Israel is proclaimed.

5 June 1948. The housewife's choice, *My Love*, owned by the Aga Khan, wins the Derby.

5 July 1948. National Health Service comes into being. It offers free medical care to whole population.

14 August 1948. Don Bradman is bowled for a duck at the Oval in his last Test innings.

17 Sept 1948. UN mediator, Count Folke Bernadotte, is murdered by Jewish terrorists.

3 Nov 1948. Harry Truman beats the polls and Thomas Dewey and remains President.

15 Jan 1949. Durban is hit by worst riots in South Africa's history: 106 die.

18 March 1949. Eight Western nations agree to form a new defence alliance known as the North Atlantic Treaty Organization (NATO).

25 March 1949. Laurence Olivier's Hamlet wins five Oscars.

2 April 1949. Coloured lights, floodlighting and neon signs light up after 10-year ban.

24 April 1949. Chocolate and sweet rationing ends.

2 May 1949. Arthur Miller wins the Pulitzer Prize for his play *Death of a Salesman*.

12 May 1949. Berlin blockade is lifted.

30 June 1949. "Gorgeous Gussie" Moran shocks Wimbledon with her lace-trimmed panties.

18 Sept 1949. The pound is devalued by 30 per cent.

1 Oct 1949. Mao Tse Tung proclaims China a Communist republic.

30 Dec 1949. "Crawfie", former royal governess, enrages royal family by publishing her memoirs.

King and Queen mark silver wedding

London, 26 April 1948

The king and queen celebrated their silver wedding today with a thanksgiving service at St Paul's Cathedral where the Archbishop of Canterbury made the point that Britain had much to give thanks for: "The nation and the empire bless God that He has set such a family at the seat of our royalty." The service over, the obviously happy couple set out on a 22-mile drive through the streets of London in an open coach. Cheers greeted them wherever they went. Later, they both broadcast to the nation. The queen declared her conviction that married life provides the foundation on which all the best in the life of the nation is built. "Looking back over the last 25 years and to my own happy childhood, I realise more and more that wonderful sense of security and happiness which comes from a loving home."

Their own lives are shining examples of what she preaches. Coming, unwillingly, to the throne they have been sustained in peace and war by their affection for each other and have rebuilt the monarchy into a family affair in which they are loved as well as honoured. Throughout these 25 years the king has shown reserves of courage which few suspected he possessed, but he could not have done it without her support, determination and fierce protection. He may have been born royal but it is she who has given him the will to reign.

Special service held in St Paul's Cathedral to celebrate 25 years of marriage.

City turns out to watch the King and Queen's procession drive to St Paul's.

Roosevelt memorial unveiled in London

London, 12 April 1948

The queen attended the unveiling of a statue of President Roosevelt today in Grosvenor Square, which, occupied by the US embassy and several other American agencies, is known to Londoners as "Little America". Most of the money for the statue, erected on a lawn in the middle of the square, was subscribed by ordinary people in honour of the man who did so much to help Britain in the dark days of the war. She, no doubt, recalled the momentous royal visit to the president in Washington in 1939 which helped seal the "special relationship" between the two countries.

The Queen in Grosvenor Square.

Olympic Games are held at White City

London, 14 August 1948

Twelve years and two abandoned Olympic Games after Hitler's 1936 propaganda spectacular in Berlin, London has been the venue this summer for the first games since the war ended. Held amid the strictures of post-war austerity, they have been run on a shoe-string but they have been enormously successful. America won 38 gold medals while Britain could only manage three in rowing and yachting. However the Olympic spirit was maintained by the Dutch housewife Fanny Blankers-Koen, 30, who won four gold medals.

Joy at first grandchild is marred by King's illness

King's frailty shows at Garter ceremony

The Order of the Garter celebrates its 600th anniversary at Windsor Castle.

London, 30 April 1948

There is concern about the king's health. At the 600th anniversary service of the Order of the Garter held at Windsor Castle this month it was noted, amidst all the pageantry, that he was looking drawn and frail. Never robust, he was exhausted by the war and has not properly recovered but it is feared there is something more seriously wrong with him. He is a heavy smoker and for some time he has suffered from poor circulation in his right leg. He sometimes bangs his leg against his desk to restore feeling in it.

Prince Charles is christened at the Palace

London, 15 December 1948

The king and queen's first grandchild was christened Charles Philip Arthur George by the Archbishop of Canterbury in a private ceremony at Buckingham Palace today. The infant defied tradition and slept peacefully through the ceremony. Few babies have had such a royal cast of godparents: His grandfather, King George VI; his great-grandmother, Queen Mary; his aunt, Princess Margaret; his paternal great-grandmother, Victoria, Dowager Marchioness of Milford Haven; his great-uncle, the Hon. David Bowes Lyon; Lady Brabourne, daughter of Earl Mountbatten of Burma; and his great-uncles, King Haakon of Norway and Prince George of Greece. It was a grand occasion and Queen Mary marked it by "giving the baby a silver gilt cup & cover which George III had given to a godson in 1780, so that I gave a present from my great-grandfather to my great-grandson 168 years later." More important to the queen as

Proud grannie holds the baby.

she cradled her infant grandson in her arms was that her husband appeared to be making a good recovery. He had been allowed out of bed for the christening and the queen had hung new pictures in his Audience Chamber to please him when he left his bedroom.

Serious illness raises fears for King's life

London, 12 March 1949

The queen spent one of the most worrying days of her life today as the king underwent an operation in a specially fitted surgery in Buckingham Palace. It had been hoped that his long period of bed-rest would ease the thickening of the arteries in his legs and, indeed, he was able to enjoy Christmas at Sandringham and have a day's shooting. But his condition has worsened, he is frail and there has been danger of gangrene in his right leg. In the operation he has undergone today, a right lumbar sympathectomy, Professor James Learmonth has cut the nerve which controls the blood vessels in the leg, opening and closing them rather like a thermostat. Now they will remain open, allowing maximum circulation. The problem is that with no way of restricting the blood supply the leg will feel excessively hot on a warm day. It appears the operation has been a success but, at 54, with a lifetime of heavy smoking behind him there is still danger of a thrombosis or some other life-threatening complication. He will have to severely restrict his activities and must avoid overstressing himself, physically and mentally. This means that the queen must shoulder even more of the royal duties. She will do this cheerfully – as long as her Bertie gets better.

Enjoying a quiet evening at home.

Another picture for the album as royal family rejoices at Charles' christening.

Anne, a little sister for Prince Charles

London, 15 August 1950

Princess Elizabeth gave birth to a daughter, who will be called Anne, at Clarence House at 11.50 this morning. Prince Philip, who is serving with the Mediterranean fleet, flew home for the birth of his daughter. He has double cause to celebrate today for he was promoted Lieutenant Commander this morning and given command of his first ship, the frigate HMS *Magpie*.

The princess has been enjoying the life of a naval officer's wife in Malta. For the first time she has been able to behave almost like any other young married woman, going to sports events and beach parties, haggling in the market, driving her own car, and giving and attending small dinner parties with other naval couples. True, there is always a detective keeping a discreet eye on her safety, but compared with her previous life, this is freedom. She hopes to return to Malta as soon as Anne is old enough. In the midst of all this happiness, however, there is a worm of anxiety. The king has not fully recovered his strength after his operation and has remained at

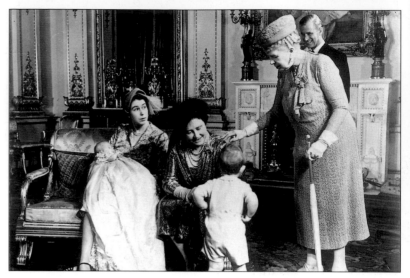

Prince Charles plays with grannie and great-grandma at Anne's christening.

Balmoral to convalesce rather than return to London for the birth of his second grandchild. Queen Elizabeth, torn between staying with her husband or being with her daughter, chose to be at the birth but has spent much time on the telephone to Balmoral, giving the king the news and checking on his health. Remembering what pleasure she and the king have enjoyed from their daughters, she is delighted with the baby. The crowd outside Clarence House have been given the news. Royal salutes have been fired in Hyde Park. And among the honours offered the new baby is membership of the Automobile Association, which made her its millionth member when she was less than one hour old.

War breaks out in South Korea

Seoul, 25 June 1950

Communist North Korea launched a massive surprise attack on the independent southern half of this divided country at dawn today. Tanks and troops stormed over the border, sweeping away the unprepared South Koreans, while landing craft sailed down the coast to land troops behind the lines and bombers raided the capital's airfield. Within a few hours of crossing the 38th Parallel, the agreed border, the North Koreans had occupied all the territory north of the Imjin River. Reports say their Russian-supplied tanks are only 12 miles from Seoul. The invasion has caused consternation in the West. Prime Minister Clement Attlee and President Harry Truman are in conference with their senior military and diplomatic officers. The UN Security Council has summoned an emergency meeting and all the indications are that help will be rushed to South Korea.

A sick King goes to favourite variety show

London, November 1950

The king, continuing his slow recovery, has had a night out with his family at his favourite show, the Royal Command Variety performance at Covent Garden. This is the one night a year when he can relax at the theatre and enjoy the comedians, magicians, singers and dancers going through their routines. This is very much his sort of entertainment and the comedians, like the old royal jesters, have a certain licence to make reference to the occupants of the royal box. But they all end their acts with a bow to the box.

A night out with the comedians and the jugglers at the London Palladium.

Looking to the future at Festival of Britain

King and Queen are welcomed to the festival by the director, Gerald Barry.

London, 4 May 1951
The king and queen opened the Festival of Britain a hundred years to the day after Queen Victoria opened the Great Exhibition. Built on bomb sites along the south bank of the Thames, it is seen by the government as "the people giving themselves a pat on the back". A Dome of Discovery curves over the area while the Skylon, an elegant pencil of aluminium, points the way to the stars. The Royal Festival Hall will provide London with a permanent concert hall when the festival ends. The king and queen along with Queen Mary, now in a wheelchair, thoroughly enjoyed their visit but it was noted once again how gaunt the king looked.

Elizabeth tours gardens in heart of London

London, 2 August 1951
The queen, who gets so much pleasure out of gardening, undertook one of her favourite duties today, touring London's small backgardens and presenting schools with prizes for their splendidly kept gardens. The joint winners this year in the competition sponsored by the London Garden Society were the Nelson Secondary School, Walworth, and Hither Green Senior Boys School. The queen was delighted when she was presented with a bunch of sweet peas grown by a green-fingered schoolboy.

A schoolboy gardener presents a bunch of sweet peas to a sweet lady.

The Queen pays a Festival visit to Cardiff

The Queen is introduced to the Welch Regiment's inquisitive mascot.

Cardiff, May 1951
The queen has learnt over the years the dangers of getting too close to military mascots. Horses tend to eat bouquets and on one occasion an RAF pelican tried to swallow her handbag. She kept a wary eye therefore on the goat mascot of the Welch Regiment when he was introduced to her during her visit to Cardiff to attend the city's Festival of Britain celebrations. These celebrations are taking place all over the country and the queen is attending as many as she can, taking the place of the king in order not to disappoint the people. She carries out these duties with that famous smile lighting up her face despite her anxiety over the king's health.

Variety show piped into King's sick room

London, 14 November 1951
The queen went to the Royal Variety show without the king this year. She put on a brave face and smiled the famous smile but, for once, anxiety was etched in her face and the laughs did not ring out as usual from the royal box. The king, however, was determined not to miss the show and had it piped into his bedroom. He is said to have enjoyed it and to be making good progress. There is still much apprehension about his condition following the operation to remove his left lung on September 23 and he has still not been told that there was a cancerous tumour in his lung. The queen knows but maintains her facade of cheerfulness, spending many hours with him when not occupied with royal duties. Among the few good things that have happened this sad autumn is the tour of Canada by Princess Elizabeth and Prince Philip which was a tremendous success. They went on to visit President Truman in Washington and the president wrote to the king: "We've just had a visit from a lovely young lady and her personable husband ..." The king's condition was such, however, that the princess's private secretary carried with him the papers necessary for her accession if her father died while she was away,

Putting on a brave face at the theatre. ▷

Churchill becomes Premier again

London, 26 October 1951
Winston Churchill is Prime Minister again following the general election which has given the Tories an over-all majority of 17, and tonight he is forming his first peacetime government. He will not find it easy to lead the country; he is 77, two years ago suffered a slight stroke and the problems facing the country now are far different to those he sur-mounted so triumphantly in the war. But when he accepted the king's commission today, he seemed reju-venated and the two battle-scarred veterans greeted each other warmly.

A day at the races for the Queen

The Queen gives her jockey a tip.

Sandown Park, December 1951
The king is making good progress and the queen, accompanied by Princess Margaret, has been able to spend a day at Sandown Park, one of her favourite racecourses. Racing is very much in her blood, the Bowes Lyons being notable horsemen and owners. She prefers national hunt racing to the flat and loves the atmo-sphere of the small courses. Even in the most wintry conditions with sleet slicing across the course she will go down to the paddock to inspect the horses before a race and chat to the jockeys. Above all she loves the horses themselves. She has been known to ring up her trainer, Peter Cazalet, and ask, "How are my dar-lings?" The royal family will gather at Sandringham for their traditional Christmas, but this year, fearing that the king will not be strong enough to deliver his Christmas Day broad-cast live, she is insisting that he pre-record it, line by painful line.

1952 - 1953

1 Jan 1952. Headmasters criticise the new GCE exams, claiming the standard is too high for some pupils.

10 Jan 1952. Captain Carlsen ends his 12-day solitary struggle to save his sinking freighter, the *Flying Enterprise*.

20 Jan 1952. Prime Minister Mossadegh denounces Iran's 1857 friendship treaty with Britain.

21 Feb 1952. Elizabeth Taylor marries Michael Wilding.

20 Feb 1952. British skater Jeanette Altwegg wins the Olympic gold medal for figure skating.

21 March 1952. Humphrey Bogart wins the Oscar for best actor for his role in *The African Queen*.

27 March 1952. The cheese ration is to be cut to an ounce a week.

12 April 1952. General Eisenhower says he will resign from the army if he is nominated as Republican presidential candidate.

26 April 1952. French forces are heavily engaged with Communist guerrillas in Vietnam.

2 May 1952. The jet era for passenger transport begins when a Comet airliner leaves London on its flight to Johannesburg.

3 May 1952. Newcastle United become the first team since 1891 to win the FA Cup two years running, beating Arsenal 1-0.

16 May 1952. The principle of equal pay for women doing the same jobs as men is given all-party support in the House of Commons.

27 May 1952. The queen gives permission for Benjamin Britten to write a Coronation opera about Elizabeth I and Essex.

11 June 1952. Denis Compton hits his 100th century.

15 June 1952. The diary of Anne Frank is published. It was written while she was hiding from the Gestapo before perishing in a concentration camp.

20 June 1952. Government announces that Zebra crossings will be marked by blinking orange beacons.

26 June 1952. Singing "God Save Africa", non-white South Africans begin a non-violent campaign against South Africa's apartheid laws.

King waves farewell to Princess Elizabeth

Is this the King's last goodbye?

Heathrow, 31 January 1952
All eyes were on the king here today when he said goodbye to Princess Elizabeth and Prince Philip before they flew off, in his stead, on an ar-duous five month tour of Australia and New Zealand by way of Africa. He seemed reluctant to let them go. After they had all taken a glass of champagne in the VIP lounge, he followed them into the aircraft for a final goodbye and then, as the Argonaut taxied down the runway, he stood, bare-headed in the bitter wind, waving until it was a speck in the distance. Only then could the queen persuade him to go into the warmth of the airport. The people around him, Churchill among them, noticed how gaunt he was and that his face had taken on the glare with which he disguises emotion. The queen, recognising the signs, put her hand gently on his arm and he smiled sadly at her. It was a moving, intimate moment for those who no-ticed it, revealing the extent of their love and understanding for each other. Both of them know he is walking with death and that he real-ises he may never see his "Lilibet" again. What the doctors fear most is a sudden thrombosis. Tomorrow he is going to Sandringham, the place he likes best, in the hope that the bracing east coast air will help build up his strength. He cannot manage a full scale shoot anymore but plans to take part in a rough shoot for rabbits and hares.

King George, his face etched with illness, raises his hat to well-wishers.

King George dies in his sleep, the nation mourns

The royal family gathers at Sandringham and throughout the nation people meet in silent groups to read the headlines as news spreads of the King's death.

Sandringham, 6 February 1952

King George VI is dead, the nation mourns a good man and the queen is distraught over the loss of her beloved Bertie. He had enjoyed yesterday, taking part in an informal "Keepers' Day" shoot and killing a fast-running hare with his last shot of the day. Pleasantly tired, he dined with the queen and Princess Margaret and went to bed just before 11 pm. Sometime during the night the thrombosis the doctors feared killed him in his sleep. At 7.30 this morning his valet, James MacDonald, took him his early-morning cup of tea. The king was dead. His life had been dedicated to duty in the face of the utmost difficulties. He had struggled against his shyness and speech impediment and, never wanting or expecting to be king, had been content with his happy family life with his wife and two young daughters. Thrust, untrained for the task, onto the throne by his feckless brother's abdication, his first heavy duty had been to restore the nation's faith in the monarchy. Then, faced almost immediately by the most awful war the world has ever seen, he

gave his utmost to lead the nation to victory. In a broadcast today, his wartime comrade in arms, Winston Churchill, said of him: "Never for a moment did he fail in that duty." A terrible war over, the monarchy not only secure but loved, he should have been able to relax at last. Alas, he was so worn out by the time victory was won, his final years were blighted by ill-health and he was never able to regain the contentment of his early married life. Throughout all his struggles, his wife has been at his side, smiling, calming and encouraging, but fiercely protective. Despised by the Duke and Duchess of Windsor as "Cookie", she outgunned and outstayed them when they tried to return to London. In his broadcast today Churchill described her as "that most valiant woman". She will need all her valour now for she has lost the man she was unwilling to marry but round whom she has built her life. Suddenly, she is no longer the queen. Her daughter now takes precedence, but the loss of pomp and circumstance means little to her. What matters is that she has lost the man she loved.

Princess Elizabeth now Queen Elizabeth II

Heathrow, 7 February 1952

The young woman who left this airport as Princess Elizabeth a week ago, returned to it today as Queen Elizabeth II. As her aircraft rolled to a halt three grave figures waited to pay homage to her – Winston Churchill, Clement Attlee and Anthony Eden – statesmen who had served her father and would now serve her. She had actually become queen while watching rhinoceros at a waterhole beneath the Treetops hotel, built in the branches of a giant fig tree in Kenya's Aberdare Forest. It was a shocked reporter who gave the news of the king's death to her Private Secretary, Martin Charteris, and it fell to her husband to break the news to her. She was back in Clarence House by four this afternoon and shortly afterwards her first caller arrived. It was Queen Mary. "Her old grannie and subject," said that indomitable woman, "must be the first to kiss her hand." The new queen must now attend her Accession Council. In the meanwhile, her

sorrowing mother, whose new title must be decided, remains at Sandringham where the king lies in state in the little family church, his coffin draped in the royal standard.

Churchill awaits the new Queen.

89

Big Ben tolls as King George VI is borne through

Windsor, 16 February 1952

King George VI was laid to rest in the vault of his ancestors at St George's Chapel here today with all the pomp and tradition of monarchy. He had lain first in the church at Sandringham, watched over by his gamekeepers and estate workers like a country squire. Then he had been taken in his coffin of Sandringham oak to lie in state at Westminster Hall where Guards officers stood at the four corners of the catafalque and more than 300,000 people queued for some four hours in the cold misery of austerity London to pay their last respects to the diffident man they had come to love.

Finally, he made his last journey through the streets of his capital on a gun-carriage pulled by his sailors, with men of the Household Cavalry marching in slow time to funereal music, to Paddington where the royal train was waiting to carry him to Windsor. There were poignant moments. As the cortege left Westminster, Big Ben rang out, tolling once a minute to mark the 56 years of the king's life. Then, as the gun carriage passed Marlborough House, the figure of Queen Mary, too frail to attend the funeral, could be seen at a window bowing with great dignity in farewell to her son.

St George's Chapel was filled with members of Europe's royal families and statesmen from all over the world. The coffin was heaped with flowers. One wreath, from Churchill, bore the Victoria Cross citation: "For Valour". Garter King-of-Arms recited the roll of titles of the dead monarch over the open tomb. Then, as the coffin was lowered into the vault to the sound of muffled drums, the new queen took a handful of earth from a small silver bowl and scattered it over the coffin while Lord Chamberlain held up his staff of office, snapped it in two and threw it into the vault.

Perhaps even more impressive than the pageantry of the funeral was the way in which ordinary people throughout the country observed two minutes silence during the burial. The deep quiet which fell on the nation was indicative of the affection and respect in which the king was held. Churchill with his "For Valour" has, as usual, expressed the mood of the people.

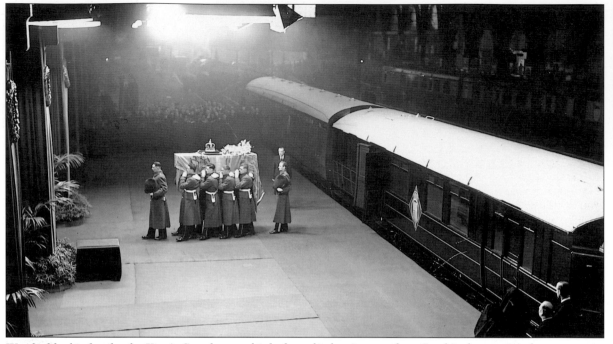

Watched by his family, the King's Guards carry his body on his last journey from Sandringham to London.

Bluejackets pull the gun-carriage with the King's coffin through London on the way to his burial at Windsor Castle.

the sad, silent streets of his capital

London, 18 February 1952

The widowed queen is determined to do everything in her power to help her daughter begin her reign. To avoid confusion between the two Queen Elizabeths she has announced that in the future she will be known as "Queen Elizabeth, The Queen Mother". With loving disrespect the people have immediately shortened it to "The Queen Mum". She has also sent a special message to the country: "He loved you all, every one of you, most truly. That, you know, was what he always tried to tell you in his yearly message at Christmas. Throughout our married life we have tried, the King and I, to fulfil with all our hearts and all our strength the great task of service that was laid upon us. My only wish now is that I may be allowed to continue the work that we sought to do together. I commend to you our dear daughter. Give her your loyalty and devotion: in the great and lonely station to which she has been called she will need your protection and your love."

Behind her dignified public countenance, however, there is pain and bitterness. The iciness with which she treated the Duke of Windsor at the funeral was noticeable and the duke, who travelled from France to take his place among the family mourners, was not invited to the funeral lunch. She is convinced that by abdicating he laid upon her husband stresses which she believes killed him. In effect she blames her early widowhood on the duke.

She has, however, been comforted by the astonishing world-wide reaction to her husband's death. The grief in the Commonwealth countries is to be expected but in republican America, Congress passed a resolution of sympathy and adjourned as a mark of respect. Secretary of State Dean Acheson read a prepared tribute at a press conference then added: "The King's outstanding quality has been his selfless dedication to duty." Rene Massigli, the French Ambassador to London, has written to his Foreign Minister: "... brought to the throne in a climate of dynastic and constitutional crisis, George VI has died leaving to his daughter a throne more stable than England has known throughout almost her entire history".

King George lies in state guarded by his Yeomen in Westminster Abbey.

Three queens in deepest mourning for their son, husband and father.

Black Watch leaves for Korean war

Fife, May 1952

The Queen Mother, colonel of her family regiment, the Black Watch, has flown here to bid the regiment Godspeed as it leaves to join the Commonwealth division fighting in Korea. This is her first public engagement since the death of the king and her friends are glad to see her out and about again for, still overwhelmed with grief, she has shut herself away in Birkhall, the house on the Balmoral estate she and her husband lived in during the early happy years of their marriage. She dresses in black and refuses to entertain, seeing nobody except her closest friends and her immediate family. Fear is growing that, like Queen Victoria after the death of her Bertie, she will become a professional widow. It has taken something as personal as the Black Watch going to war to bring her out.

First duty since her husband's death.

Queen Mary dies at Malborough House

London, 24 March 1953

Queen Mary, the regal embodiment of a past era, has died, aged 85, at Marlborough House. She had been a queen since 1910 when her husband, George V, acceded to the throne. She was a woman of indomitable will and discipline. Churchill says of her: "She looked like a queen and she acted like a queen."

3 Feb 1953. Sea defences collapse and floods devastate East coast: 125 known drowned, 500 missing.

5 March 1953. Josef Stalin, dictator of the Soviet empire, dies of cerebral haemorrhage. He was 73.

26 March 1953. Dr Jonas Salk has developed a vaccine against polio.

6 June 1953. Gordon Richards becomes the first jockey to be knighted.

19 June 1953. Soviet atom spies Ethel and Julius Rosenburg go to the electric chair in Sing Sing.

20 June 1953. Soviet tanks crush workers' uprising in East Berlin.

27 July 1953. The Korean War ends after three years of bloody fighting.

12 Sept 1953. John F Kennedy marries Jacqueline Bouvier.

2 Oct 1953. The latest fashion in footwear is the stiletto heel.

31 Dec 1953. *The Goon Show* is the radio programme of the year.

11 Jan 1954. All BOAC Comet jetliners are grounded after second mysterious crash. Is metal fatigue to blame?

6 May 1954. Medical student Roger Bannister breaks the four-minute-mile barrier. He clocks 3 minutes 59.4 seconds.

8 May 1954. The French bastion at Dien Bien Phu falls to the Viet Cong.

2 June 1954. Lester Piggott, 18 years old, riding *Never Say Die*, becomes the youngest Derby winner.

1 July 1954. Britain's rabbits are in danger of being wiped out by a new disease, myxomatosis.

3 July 1954. Housewives burn their ration books as government announces the end of all rationing after 14 years.

24 Sept 1954. A temple to the Roman god Mithras is discovered near the Mansion House.

30 Nov 1954. Sir Winston Churchill celebrates his 80th birthday. Presented with a portrait of himself by the merciless Graham Sutherland, he says: "It certainly combines force and candour."

31 Dec 1954. William Golding's *Lord of the Flies* is the book of the year.

Vivat Regina! Elizabeth II is crowned

Queen Elizabeth, the Queen Mother, looks after a bored Prince Charles as he watches his mother's coronation.

Crown and sceptre for the Queen.

Crowned: the new monarch, wearing her diadem, occupies the royal throne.

London, 2 June 1953

Queen Elizabeth II was crowned today in Westminster Abbey. Some 8,000 people filled the abbey to proclaim their allegiance to their "undoubted queen" while, for the first time, millions watched the ceremony in their own homes through the medium of televison. The streets were lined by nearly three million, many of whom had waited all night in the rain and cold to watch the brilliant procession. Rarely has there been such a display of national pride and affection. Roar after roar of thunderous applause followed the royal coach as the queen, in a robe of royal velvet, wearing the Imperial State Crown and carrying the Orb and Sceptre, drove back to Buckingham Palace, to appear surrounded by her family on the balcony of the palace. The Queen Mother, who for so long has played a central role in the great ceremonies of state, today played the role of grandmother, restraining the lively four-year-old Prince Charles when he leant too far over the balcony to watch his mother take the Coronation Oath.

Tonight the sky has cleared, there are fireworks and street parties and the queen has broadcast her pledge to the people: "Throughout all my life and with all my heart I shall strive to be worthy of your trust."

British expedition conquers Everest

London, 2 June 1953

Cheers rang through the coronation crowds when it became known that the New Zealander Edmund Hillary and Sherpa Tensing had conquered Mount Everest. The success of the British expedition led by Colonel John Hunt is seen as a good omen for the start of the queen's reign. The two climbers reached the summit last Friday but news of their success and safe descent did not reach Khatmandu until yesterday.

Margaret and Townsend admit their love

The lovers together at a fair.

London, 14 June 1953

Once again the workings of the human heart are causing dismay and unhappiness in the royal family. The whole world now knows that Princess Margaret is in love with Group Captain Peter Townsend. Millions of people watching the coronation ceremony on their television sets saw the radiant princess go up to the handsome fighter ace, and affectionately, intimately, brush a loose thread from the breast pocket of his uniform. The next day American newspapers carried photographs of that moment and the story of their affair. The British press, customarily reticent over royal matters, said nothing until today when the *People* used the device of printing the stories from abroad and denying them in order to break the news. The queen and Queen Mother have known about it for some time, and Margaret has told them that she wants to marry Townsend, who now is Comptroller of Clarence House where she lives with her mother. They would make a handsome couple, but Townsend is a divorced man with children whose wife is still living and such a marriage would cause scandal. The queen has, therefore, asked Margaret to wait until she is 25 in two years time.

Queen Mother takes care of Margaret

London, 30 June 1953

The Queen Mother has turned away from her own grief to comfort her younger daughter, caught in the toils of a seemingly impossible love affair. The "Queen Mum" has seen it all before with her brother-in-law and Mrs Simpson and knows the unhappiness such affairs bring. She is also a firm believer in the sanctity of marriage but is doing nothing to affect the course of the romance, merely offering comfort and solace. Today mother and daughter have set out on a de Havilland Comet – the world's first passenger jet – to pay an official visit to Rhodesia. They have flown in the Comet before, on a short trip when the Queen Mother took the controls and

Down to earth after Comet flight.

Dressmaker Norman Hartnell presents his spring collection to his royal clients.

frightened test pilot "Catseyes" Cunningham by pushing its speed up to the danger zone. This time they are going, sedately, to open the centenary celebrations of the birth of Cecil Rhodes. The visit is planned partly to ease the Queen Mother back into the royal business and partly to separate Margaret and Townsend. Rumours suggest he is to return to active duty and will be posted to Brussels as air attaché.

Warm welcome home for Queen Mother

London, 24 November 1954

The Queen Mother came home to a rousing reception today after another triumphant visit to the United States and Canada. When she was invited to make the tour she was reluctant: "Who is going to be interested in the middle-aged widow of a king?" She went only because the visit was to receive money raised in memory of her husband to enable young people from the Commonwealth to be educated in America. As she feared, the visit started slowly but after she was presented with the cheque at a televised dinner, crowds turned out to cheer her wherever she went. "Of all the many reasons for welcoming Queen Elizabeth, the Queen Mother," wrote the *New York Times*, "the pleasantest is that she is so nice." Her welcome was even warmer in Canada, a country she describes as a "magnificent adventure in human brotherhood". And today she was welcomed home by adoring crowds. It would seem that her rehabilitation is complete.

The royal clan gathers to greet the Queen Mother on her return from America.

The Queen Mother buys the semi-derelict Castle of Mey in Caithness. She intends to restore it as her new hideaway home in Scotland.

8 Feb 1955. Nikita Khrushchev emerges as the undisputed leader of the Soviet Union.

5 April 1955. Sir Winston Churchill, old and frail, has his last audience with the queen and hands over premiership to Sir Anthony Eden.

11 June 1955. Eighty people die when three cars crash at 150mph on the Le Mans track.

14 August 1955. Exhibition of Annigoni's stunning portrait of the queen breaks all attendance records at the Royal Academy.

30 Sept 1955. Greek Cypriots riot against British control as extremist group EOKA steps up its campaign for union with Greece.

30 Sept 1955. Actor James Dean dies in car smash at 24.

18 March 1956. Nikita Khrushchev makes a secret speech to the 20th Party Congress bitterly attacking Stalin.

29 June 1956. Playwright Arthur Miller marries the world's pinup, Marilyn Monroe.

26 Oct 1956. Hungarians rise against Soviet domination.

6 Nov 1956. Anglo-French forces invade Egypt following Nasser's seizure of the Suez Canal.

10 Jan 1957. Harold MacMillan succeeds Sir Anthony Eden as Premier.

7 Feb 1957. Bill Haley and his Comets take London by storm.

25 March 1957. France, West Germany, Italy, Belgium, Holland and Luxembourg sign the Treaty of Rome, setting up the Common Market.

31 August 1957. Lord Altrincham writes magazine article attacking the queen: "a priggish schoolgirl, captain of the hockey team".

4 Oct 1957. Russia launches the Sputnik satellite into orbit and opens the Space Age.

6 Feb 1958. Plane crash at Munich destroys Manchester United, the Busby Babes.

18 March 1958. The last debutantes to be presented at Court make their curtseys to the queen.

9 Sept 1958. Race riots flare in Notting Hill Gate.

5 Dec 1958. Britain's first stretch of motorway, the eight-mile Preston by-pass, is opened by Harold MacMillan who says it is "a token of what was to follow".

Margaret renounces Peter Townsend

London, 31 October 1955

After two weeks of soul-searching amid world-wide speculation, Princess Margaret tonight put duty before love and, eyes brimming with tears, declared that she would not marry Peter Townsend, the glamourous Battle of Britain hero she first met as a teenager when he became equerry to her late father. At the age of 25 she could now marry the divorced Townsend without the permission of the queen. She would, however, have to wait a year, lose her payments from the civil list and her position as third in line to the throne. Even so, when Margaret and Townsend met again a fortnight ago and discovered they were still in love, she was determined to go ahead with the marriage; even dinner with the Archbishop of Canterbury failed to move her. Last week, however, her disapproving sister told her that Prime Minister Anthony Eden had said she would have to

A tearful Princess Margaret after announcing she is giving up her love.

marry abroad and stay there, at least for a few years. Under the combined pressure of family, church and state, she finally crumbled. In her statement she said: "Mindful of the church's teaching that Christian marriage is indissoluble and conscious of my duty to the Commonwealth, I have resolved to put these considerations before others ..." She paid tribute to her lover's "unfailing support and devotion".

President Nasser seizes Suez Canal

Alexandria, 26 July 1956

Just two weeks after the last British troops left the Canal Zone under the terms of the 1954 Anglo-Egyptian agreement, President Nasser has "nationalised" the Anglo-French controlled Suez Canal Company, in effect seizing the vital life line for oil supplies to Europe. The British and French governments are outraged by Nasser's arbitrary action but the Egyptian people are dancing in the streets. Speaking here on the fourth anniversary of his overthrow of King Farouk, Nasser said if the "imperialist powers" did not like it they could "choke to death on their fury". He threatened to imprison Canal employees, many of whom are British, if they try to quit their jobs and he boasted: "We shall industrialise Egypt and compete with the West. We are marching from strength to strength." However, his seizure of the Canal seems not to be part of a considered policy but a reaction to the refusal by the US and Britain to finance the building of the Aswan High Dam, itself a reaction to his $200 million arms deal with the Communist bloc.

Royals turn out for Windsor polo matches

Windsor, Summer 1956

The Queen Mother, lover of anything to do with horses, has become an enthusiastic follower of polo. She often watches matches at Smith's Lawn in Windsor Great Park, headquarters of the Duke of Edinburgh's newly founded Household Brigade Polo Club. The duke is a vigorous and skilful player and the royal family regularly turn out to watch his team. Their presence along with the young guards officers and hard-riding foreign players is rapidly turning Smith's Lawn into one of the most fashionable places at which to be seen at the weekend. This does not bother the "Queen Mum". She is concerned with the ponies and looking after Prince Charles, now 7, and any other young royals who happen to be around.

Queen Mother keeps a watchful eye on Prince Charles and King Hussein.

Queen Mother returns to the dance floor

She could have danced all night ...

London, November 1956
The Queen Mother dances with an elderly but still dashing and elegant cavalry officer, and her friends are delighted that she has recovered sufficiently from her grief over the death of her husband to take to the dance floor again. She has always loved dancing, especially the noisy, high-spirited reels danced at Scottish country house balls. Among her favourites is the annual Ghillies' Ball at Balmoral where she threads her way expertly through the intricacies of the eightsomes. She and her brother David were taught by a dancing master when they were young, but she took to the lessons a foot-tapping exuberance which she has never lost.

Nice to be beside the seaside Down Under

Queen Mother attends Australia's biggest surf carnival on Manly Beach.

Keeping up with regimental traditions

London, 1 March 1957
The Queen Mother, standing in for the queen as colonel-in-chief of the Welch Guards, proudly wore her St David's Day leek, emblem of the regiment, when she reviewed the guardsmen today at Chelsea Barracks. As colonel-in-chief of 13 regiments and corps, honorary colonel of four others and commandant-in-chief of the women's services, the WRNS, the WRAC, and the WRAF, she appreciates the importance military units attach to rituals which often date from some half-forgotten battle. But the leeks of the Welch Guards and the shamrock of the Irish Guards are different. They represent the national pride which imbues the regiments and makes them so formidable in battle.

The Queen Mother is given a leek by the Welch Guards in a St David's Day ceremony at Chelsea Barracks.

London, March 1958
The Queen Mother has been welcomed home from her gruelling world tour with a banquet at the Guildhall where the royal family, politicians and city dignitaries gathered to thank her for another brilliantly successful display of the "Queen Mum" magic. Setting out in January, she has visited Canada, Honolulu, Fiji, New Zealand, Australia and Tasmania. Enthusiastic crowds have surrounded her wherever she has been – even in Launceston, Tasmania, where gale-force winds swept the hats off the ladies waiting for a royal introduction. Informality was the keynote of the tour. Much to the alarm of her officials, she went "walkabout" in the huge crowds, shaking hands and chatting. She hugged a koala bear in Brisbane, enjoyed the surf carnival at Manly Beach and when she flew from Perth, schoolchildren formed a living tableau of the map of Australia to wish her "Godspeed". It is now evident that far from withdrawing from public life, she has become a beloved ambassador for Britain.

A welcome at Government House.

The Queen Mother's Devon Loch is winning the Grand National ...

... but just short of the post her feet start to slip ...

... and even though she gets up and her jockey stays in the saddle ...

... ESB goes on to win. Queen Mother says 'that's racing'.

2 Jan 1959. Rebel leader Fidel Castro takes power in Cuba.

6 May 1959. Iceland and Britain wage a bloodless "Cod War."

14 Oct 1959. Errol Flynn, hell-raising swashbuckler of the silver screen, dies at 50.

3 Feb 1960. Harold MacMillan tells South Africans; "The wind of change is blowing through this continent."

5 May 1960. American U-2 spyplane is shot down by Russians over Siberia.

2 Nov 1960. Old Bailey jury decides that *Lady Chatterley's Lover*, banned for 30 years, is not obscene.

9 Nov 1960. John F Kennedy defeats Richard Nixon by narrow margin to become President of the US.

30 Jan 1961. "The Pill", an oral contraceptive for women, goes on sale in Britain.

12 April 1961. The Russian Major Yuri Gagarin, becomes the first man to fly in space.

31 August 1961. The Communists build a wall across Berlin, sealing off the Western sectors.

13 Sept 1961. Sir David Bowes Lyon dies. He was 59.

17 Sept 1961. Huge ban-the-bomb demonstration in London ends in violent clashes and 850 arrests.

4 Feb 1962. The Sunday Times publishes a "Colour Supplement". It gets a mixed reception.

31 May 1962. Israel hangs Adolf Eichmann, "transport manager" of the Holocaust.

5 August 1962. Marilyn Monroe is found dead of a drug overdose.

28 Oct 1962. World steps back from the nuclear brink when Khrushchev and Kennedy hammer out Cuban deal.

14 Jan 1963. President de Gaulle rebuffs Britain's bid to join the Common Market.

8 August 1963. A gang gets away with £1 million in "The Great Train Robbery".

22 Nov 1963. President Kennedy is assassinated as he drives with his wife in a motorcade through Dallas, Texas. Former marine, Lee Harvey Oswald, is arrested. The world is appalled.

24 Nov 1963. Lee Harvey Oswald is shot dead in Dallas police headquarters by smalltime crook Jack Ruby.

Margaret marries photographer Tony

London, 6 May 1960

Looking like a princess from a fairy-tale, Princess Margaret rode in a glass carriage through the sunshine of a perfect spring morning to Westminster Abbey today to marry photographer Antony Armstrong-Jones. Her obvious happiness radiated to the people lining the streets who cheered as she passed down the Mall beneath a 60-foot high arch of pink and white roses and crimson banners bearing the initials "M" and "A". She wore an exquisite silk dress designed by Norman Hartnell and was attended by eight brides-maids including her niece Princess Anne. The queen and Queen Mother headed the 2,000 guests in the abbey who watched the couple exchange their marriage vows before the Archbishop of Canterbury. Millions more watched the ceremony on television; what was once a semi-private state occasion can now be

The newly-weds walk hand in hand past the Queen after their wedding.

'2,000 guests'

experienced in every home in the country. After the ceremony the newly weds drove back to Buckingham Palace and then, following the wedding breakfast, drove to the Tower of London to board the royal yacht, *Britannia* which has been re-fitted for their honeymoon in the Caribbean. It has been a joyful occasion. The Queen Mother is especially happy that her younger daughter, now 29, has found someone to love. An artistic man and an excellent photographer, he is popular with the royal family and is said to share the same sense of humour as the queen. He has, however, caused concern in some quarters. Besides being a "commoner" he is in a rather "fast" London set. There was something of a scandal when his initial choice of best man was discovered by the press to have been convicted as a homosexual and he had to be replaced. None of this will matter if he succeeds in laying the ghost of Margaret's tragic love for the divorced Peter Townsend. Despite the splendour of today's occasion, there were few people in the country who did not wonder what would have happened if Margaret had been allowed to marry her dashing pilot.

Smile for the camera: Antony masterminds the official wedding photograph.

Margaret and Tony read messages of congratulation at The Royal Lodge.

Queen Mother keeps up non-stop round of work

She attends a ceremony at Belfast University, returning to the scene of one of her first royal duties soon after she married the Duke of York.

She is given a standing ovation at a gala performance of 'The Marriage of Figaro' in aid of charity at the Royal Opera House, Covent Garden.

One of her favourite sporting 'duties'. She attends Derby Day at Epsom.

This is pure pleasure. Surrounded by her family and friends she watches the Badminton Horse Trials sitting on bales of hay on a crowded farm cart.

Back to Covent Garden. She is greeted by Queen Fabiola of Belgium.

At the inaugural service of the Guards Chapel at Wellington Barracks, rebuilt after being destroyed with great loss of life by a V1 in 1944.

She is introduced to the Beatles in the backstage line-up of performers at the Royal Variety Show, which was her husband's favourite night out.

8 Feb 1964. The Beatles get a rapturous reception from thousands of teenagers when they land in New York.

7 August 1964. President Johnson receives approval from Congress to take "all necessary action" against the Communists in Vietnam.

15 Oct 1964. Nikita Khrushchev is overthrown while he is on holiday. Leonid Brezhnev takes over.

30 Jan 1965. Sir Winston Churchill is buried in a village churchyard after a state funeral in St Paul's Cathedral. He was 90.

6 April 1965. Britain sweeps the Oscars. Julie Andrews is voted best actress for *Mary Poppins* which gets five awards. *My Fair Lady* gets eight.

28 Oct 1965. Ian Brady and Myra Hindley are charged with the "Moors Murders".

8 Jan 1966. US troops launch biggest offensive in Vietnam with attack on the Viet Cong's "Iron Triangle" stronghold.

17 March 1966. Irish steeplechaser Arkle celebrates St Patrick's Day by winning the Gold Cup for the third time running.

30 July 1966. England beat Germany 4-2 at Wembley to win the World Cup.

22 Oct 1966. George Blake, sentenced to 42 years for spying for Russia, breaks out of jail and vanishes.

31 Dec 1966. Swinging London has become the fashion and rock capital of the world.

4 Jan 1967. Speed king Donald Campbell dies when his jet-powered Bluebird somersaults during record-breaking attempt on Coniston Water.

30 March 1967. RAF bombs the wreck of the tanker *Torrey Canyon* in attempt to destroy the oil fouling Cornish beaches.

7 June 1967. The queen and Queen Mother greet the Duke and Duchess of Windsor at the unveiling of a plaque in memory of Queen Mary at Marlborough House.

10 June 1967. Israel has triumphed in its Six-Day War against its Arab neighbours.

3 Dec 1967. The first transplant of a human heart is successfully carried out on Louis Washkansky by Professor Christiaan Barnard in Groote Schuur Hospital, Cape Town.

18 Dec 1967. British traitor, "Third Man" Kim Philby, is acclaimed in Moscow.

Edward's first Trooping of the Colour

The Queen in her Guards uniform holds up Prince Edward at Buckingham Palace to see the soldiers march past.

London, June 1964

The royal family followed tradition and gathered on the balcony of Buckingham Palace to watch the RAF fly-past today after the Guards had performed the ceremony of Trooping the Colour with their customary precision and panache on Horse Guards Parade. As usual, the queen, clad in her scarlet tunic and tricorne hat, had ridden side-saddle at the head of her household troops back to the palace. But this year there was an innovation: the queen held up her infant son, Prince Edward, just three months old, to show him to the people gathered outside the palace. They loved it and the "Queen Mum" looked on in delight. She now has six grandchildren: Prince Charles, Princess Anne, Prince Andrew and Prince Edward; and the two children of Princess Margaret and Lord Snowdon, Viscount Linley and the month-old Lady Sarah Armstrong-Jones. The sound of new babies crying has also been heard this year in the nurseries of the Duke and Duchess of Kent, who had their second child, Lady Helen Windsor, and of Princess Alexandra and Angus Ogilvy, who had their first child, James. It brings back memories of Glamis, full of romping children, to the Queen Mother, who is proving to be an indulgent grandmother. There has been another royal birth this year, but not one that has been publicly celebrated. The Earl of Harewood, the queen's cousin, had a son, Mark, with Patricia Tuckwell, an Australian musician.

Churchill, the old warrior, dies aged 90

London 25 January 1965

Sir Winston Churchill died today at 90, fading away like the old soldier he was, full of honours after a life of conflict. His death, although expected, has saddened the Queen Mother for their relationship, clouded at first by his support for Edward VIII during the abdication crisis, developed into one of trust and admiration during the war. She realised that his support for Edward was really support for the monarchy and that once her husband became king, Churchill was utterly loyal. For his part, he recognised her devotion to the king. Both acknowledged the other's fortitude and determination.

Nation mourns Winston Churchill.

Another sad loss for Queen Mother

Leeds, 28 March 1965

The Princess Royal, only sister of George VI, died today after collapsing while walking in the grounds of her home, Harewood Castle. She was 67. Her death will be felt keenly by the Queen Mother for they became friends before either of them married through their mutual interest in the Girl Guides movement, and Princess Mary, as she then was, provided the young Lady Elizabeth with a staunch ally inside the royal family. The Queen Mother was one of her bridesmaids when she married the Earl of Harewood.

Honouring the Commonwealth war dead

On a three-day visit to Germany.

Becklingen, Germany, 13 July 1965
The Queen Mother, who is spending three days in Germany, visited the Commonwealth War Graves cemetery here today to pay her respects to men who fell in Montgomery's advance towards Berlin in the closing stages of the war. Among the 2,402 men buried here are soldiers from regiments, both British and Canadian, with which she has close associations, airmen from Commonwealth countries who came to fight for the mother country, and prisoners of war who died in the camps. The cemetery, like all those tended by the war graves commission, is impeccably kept, with simple headstones set in the turf. Each stone is carved with the regimental badge, name, and rank of the man it commemorates. Many were heartbreakingly young. The Queen Mother, who knows what it is to lose a loved one in war, walked through their ranks, stopping occasionally to read an inscription.

Trout fishing: one of her favourite sports

After the big one in New Zealand.

New Zealand, April 1966
Thirty-nine years after her first visit to Australasia, the Queen Mother has returned for a visit which is as much nostalgic holiday as state business. She has been to Australia where she visited Prince Charles, now 17, at his new school at Timbertop in bush country 200 miles north of Melbourne. She has also been to Fiji, where, on that momentous first visit, she was given a canoe which was set up on the deck of HMS *Renown*. Now, she is back in New Zealand where she is spending as much time as possible pursuing her passion for fishing. Few things give her more pleasure than wading into an icy stream to tempt a fresh-run salmon with an expertly placed fly. Here, she is hoping to emulate her success in 1927 when she hooked a six-pound trout; but two days in her waders on North Island have produced only one small trout. "It would have been better," she said, "to get one out of the deep freeze."

Queen Mother meets the entertainers

London, 14 November 1966
Although the Queen Mother's taste has always tended towards serious music and theatre, she takes part every year in the lower-browed fun of the Royal Variety Performance which her husband liked so much. His idea of a good night out was the Crazy Gang rather than Shakespeare. What the Queen Mother does enjoy is going backstage after the show and chatting to the performers. Curiously, many of those who are nerveless when performing their acts before a packed house, get stagefright when they line up to meet her; but, as usual, she puts them at ease, especially the younger artists. This year the irrepressible Frankie Howerd and the entertainer Sammy Davis Jnr. were in the line-up. They needed no reassurance.

A tourist enjoys the chateaux of the Loire

The Loire, Summer 1967
The Queen Mother is on a private visit to France, fulfilling a long-held ambition to visit the chateaux of the Loire. Despite her major abdominal operation in December, she is tireless, wearing out the British and French officials who try to keep up with her as she does the tourist run along the lovely river inspecting the grand Renaissance palaces and their gardens. With her intimate knowledge of Glamis, Balmoral, Windsor and her own Castle of Mey, she is well able to appreciate the beauty of – and the difficulties of running – the royal residence of Amboise where Leonardo da Vinci is buried, Chenonceau, soaring over the Cher, and the grandiose chateau of François I at Chambord. She is enjoying herself hugely.

Sammy Davis Jnr. makes a courtly bow as he is presented to one of his fans.

The Queen Mother is shown the sights of the historic towns along the Loire.

Charles is invested as Prince of Wales

The royal family gathers at Caernarfon Castle for Charles' investiture.

Caernarfon, 1 July 1969
Prince Charles was invested as Prince of Wales at Caernarfon Castle today in a ceremony stage-managed by the Earl of Snowdon, Constable of the Castle. Snowdon had been preparing the ceremony for two years and it worked beautifully with the prince kneeling in front of his mother to be invested with the sword, crown, rod, ring and mantle of his new rank. He had also prepared for the ceremony with a term at University College, Aberystwyth where he studied Welsh history and learned the language, making his first public speech in Welsh a month ago. The ceremony was only the second in modern times – after his great-uncle David's in 1911 – and stems from Edward I's presentation on the same spot in 1282 of his infant son as the first English Prince of Wales. As Edward had just killed the Welsh prince Llywelyn ap Gruffudd and put an end to Welsh independence, today's ceremony has not been welcomed by Welsh nationalists. Extremists have mounted 15 bomb attacks on government and military buildings in Wales and only this morning two men were killed trying to plant a bomb. Security at the ceremony was strict, but it went off without incident. Even the sun shone.

Duke of Windsor, the King who never was, dies after long illness

Paris, 28 May 1972
The Duke of Windsor, who gave up his throne for the love of Wallis Simpson, died at his home here today of throat cancer, just one week after his niece, Queen Elizabeth, paid him a farewell visit. Although desperately ill, he insisted on leaving his bed for the occasion and rose to bow to the queen when she entered accompanied by Prince Philip and the Prince of Wales. He may have been feckless and would probably have made a bad king, but he had style. In fact, he and his wife lived in kingly style, with courtiers addressing them as "Sire" and "Your Royal Highness", liveried footmen standing behind each guest at the dinner table, the royal banner hanging from the ceiling and the house filled with royal mementos. Perhaps, now that he is dead, the Queen Mother will be able to rid herself of the bitterness which is so alien to her nature. Even as late as five years ago at the unveiling of a memorial to Queen Mary when she met them in public for the first time since the abdication she was icily formal, still blaming them for forcing her husband to assume the "intolerable burden" of being king.

The Duchess grieves for her husband.

The Duke of Windsor lies in regal state in St George's Chapel, Windsor.

Princess Anne is married to Captain Mark Phillips

London, 14 November 1973

Few people have attended as many state occasions in Westminster Abbey as the Queen Mother. Today, it was the marriage of the first of her grandchildren, Princess Anne, to Captain Mark Phillips. The princess had hoped for a quiet wedding, instead she had "the wedding of the decade", a stunning spectacle watched by more than 500 million television viewers around the world. She rode with her father in a glass coach to the abbey with people straining to catch a glimpse of her dress, made of white silk embroidered in pearls with a high neckline and Tudor-style puffed sleeves. After a sumptuous wedding breakfast at Buckingham Palace they left to spend the first night of their honeymoon at Thatched House Lodge in Richmond Park before flying to Barbados, where they will spend a few days on the famous royal yacht *Britannia*.

The Windsors and the Phillips gather at Buckingham Palace to celebrate the marriage of their daughter and son.

Duke of Gloucester: the last to die

London, 10 June 1974

The Duke of Gloucester died today at 74. He was the younger brother of Edward VIII and George VI and the last survivor of George V's six children. A soldier who preferred to avoid what he called "princing about", he became a conscientious governor-general of Australia. His death leaves the Queen Mother the sole royal survivor of the great crises of the abdication and the war.

The Duke who wanted to be a soldier.

The Queen celebrates her Silver Jubilee with service and parade

London, 7 June 1977

It is Jubilee Day and the queen is celebrating 25 years on the throne. Last night she lit a bonfire at Windsor, starting off a chain of beacons from Land's End to the Shetlands. Today has been marked by a solemn and splendid service of thanksgiving in St Paul's Cathedral. A solid wall of cheers accompanied the Gold State Coach and its escort down the Mall, through Trafalgar Square and all the way to the cathedral. After the service, the queen walked to the Guildhall for a civic lunch. The crowd, waving Union Jacks, was so dense she was late for lunch, but the "walkabout" was a tremendous success. In her speech she renewed the pledge to serve the people of the nation she had first made when she was 21. She did not, she said, "regret or retract" a word of it. The people are having their own celebrations with street and village parties being held the length and breadth of the country in a carnival atmosphere not felt since 1945. Some 4,000 parties are taking place in London alone. Today's events are the highlight of the year-long celebration which started on 6 February, the actual anniversary of her accession, but the memory of the death of her father is still painful and the queen spent that weekend quietly at Windsor. On 10 February she set out on a triumphal Jubilee tour of Australasia, returning in March to start a series of six Jubilee tours throughout Britain. On 4 May she received Loyal Addresses from both Houses of Parliament and in reply she stressed that the keynote of the Jubilee would be the unity of the nation. The celebrations are far from over. There are other tours to Canada and the West Indies and miles more to travel throughout Britain.

St Paul's Cathedral is crowded for the service marking the Silver Jubilee.

The IRA murders Lord Mountbatten

County Sligo, 27 August 1979
Earl Mountbatten of Burma was murdered by the IRA today along with his grandson, Nicholas, aged 14, and a 15-year-old boatman, Paul Maxwell, when a remote controlled bomb blew his boat *Shadow V* to matchwood as they set out on a family fishing trip. Lord Mountbatten's daughter, Lady Brabourne, her son Timothy and her mother-in-law, the Dowager Lady Brabourne, are all fighting for their lives. Mountbatten came to his Irish home, Classiebawn Castle, near the seaside village of Mullaghmore for a summer holiday with his family every year. He ignored warnings that, as a cousin of the queen, he was an IRA target. But shortly after 11.30 this morning, just as the boat left harbour, it was ripped apart by what eyewitnesses described as a "roaring explosion" which blew the boat high into the air. The party's fishing gear, anoraks and plimsolls floated on the

Lord Mountbatten sets out on Shadow V, the boat in which he died.

water as the bodies were recovered. A great-grandchild of Queen Victoria, Mountbatten was a dashing destroyer captain, became supreme Allied commander in South-East Asia and was the last Viceroy of In-

dia. He enjoyed a unique position in the royal family, having brought up his nephew, Prince Philip, and acted as matchmaker in Philip's marriage to Elizabeth. Latterly he has been mentor to Prince Charles.

Queen Mother unveils statue of 'Monty'

London, 6 June 1980
On this, the anniversary of D-Day, the Queen Mother unveiled a statue of Field Marshal Viscount Montgomery in Whitehall, paying tribute to the man who led the Eighth Army to victory over Rommel at Alamein

and commanded the invading force on D-Day. There was a splendid turn-out of bemedalled old warriors in the spring sunshine and the "Queen Mum" was obviously at home with them as they refought old battles under "Monty's" stern eye.

Paying honour to the memory of the man who won the Desert War.

London, 4 March 1980. The Queen Mother shows today that she has lost none of her skill on the snooker table when she opens the Mayflower Youth Club. She apologises however, "I'm afraid I'm a bit out of practise at this game." And one of the boys replies: "Cor! Wish I could play as good as that."

Fairy tale marriage for Charles and lovely Diana

London, 29 July 1981

It was, said the Archbishop of Canterbury, "the stuff of which fairy tales are made". Nobody could possibly disagree with him as the georgeous Lady Diana Spencer walked up the aisle of St Paul's Cathedral on the arm of her father, Earl Spencer, to marry the Prince of Wales. In royal terms she is a commoner despite being an earl's daughter, just like her grandmother-in-law, the Queen Mother. But the people already see her as a fairy princess and in the fullness of time, she, too, will become queen.

The bride, just 20, was first seen by the enthusiastic crowds and the 700 million people watching their television sets all round the world as she left Clarence House, home of the Queen Mother who has taken the former kindergarten helper under her wing. Wearing a billowing cream silk gown designed by David and Elizabeth Emanuel, she waved shyly to the crowds as she drove to the cathedral in the Glass Coach. As she arrived, just one minute late, and climbed the crimson carpeted steps through banks of flowers, the Spencer family tiara sparkling in the TV lights, Prince Charles, in naval

After their marriage at St Paul's Cathedral the young couple join their families for the traditional wedding picture.

uniform, stopped joking with his brothers and took his place at the altar. They made their vows in clear, soft voices, both making, slight nervous mistakes, to the amusement of the congregation. Afterwards, he

bowed and she curtsied to the smiling queen, then drove back to Buckingham Palace for the wedding breakfast and photographs for the family album. Then they appeared on the balcony and kissed, to roars

of approval from the crowd. As they drove off to their honeymoon, a cluster of blue balloons and a sign reading "Just Married" bobbed on the back of the state landau – the work of his brothers.

The Queen Mother charms Paris again

Paris, 1982

The Queen Mother has conquered Paris just as she did on her first visit as Duchess of York over 50 years ago. Then, she and Bertie were escorted by the veteran warrior Marshal Lyautey who fell under her

spell. Today, President Mitterrand, renowned for charming the ladies, has found himself charmed by this lively, French-speaking eighty-year-old. Here on what is billed as a private visit, she is surrounded wherever she goes by adoring Parisians.

President Mitterrand welcomes the Queen Mother on her visit to Paris.

Britain wins back the Falkland Islands

The Falklands, 14 June 1982

The Argentinian invaders of the Falklands have surrendered and the Union flag is once again flying over Port Stanley. A jubilant Prime Minister Thatcher told the cheering House of Commons late tonight that the victory had been won by an operation which was "boldly planned, bravely executed and brilliantly accomplished." The end of the fighting came when British troops broke the last ring of defences round Port Stanley. After hard fighting against well dug-in defenders, the British soldiers saw large numbers of the enemy streaming back to Stanley and soon white flags began to blossom like flowers. Contact was made between a Spanish-speaking British officer and Major-General Menendez, the Argentinian commander. A cease-fire was agreed and the hopelessness of his position was explained to Menendez. Shortly afterwards the British Land Forces comman-

der, Major-General Jeremy Moore was able to signal London: "The Falkland Islands are once more under the government desired by their inhabitants. God Save the Queen." The queen has a double cause for celebration: the Falklands have been recovered and Prince Andrew, a naval helicopter pilot, has come through the conflict safely. Mrs Thatcher was greeted by cheering crowds at the entrance to Downing Street after making her Commons statement. They sang "For She's a Jolly Good Fellow". "Rule Britannia" and the National Anthem. She told them: "We had to do what we had to do. Great Britain is great again." There is a price to pay for greatness, however, and last night the names were issued of the 56 servicemen killed in the Argentinian air attacks on the landing ships *Sir Galahad* and *Sir Tristram*. The known death toll for the campaign is 255 Britons and 652 Argentinians.

6 May 1983. The "Hitler Diaries" are revealed as hoaxes after fooling historians and editors.

6 Sept 1983. Soviet Union admits shooting down Korean airliner 007 killing 269 off Sakhalin Island last week.

14 Feb 1984. Britain's Jayne Torvill and Christopher Dean win Olympic gold for ice dancing with brilliant display to Ravel's *Bolero*.

12 Oct 1984. IRA attempt to wipe out government with bomb in the Grand Hotel during Tory conference.

29 May 1985. Liverpool fans go on rampage at Heysel Stadium in Brussels. Crush leaves 38 dead. Follows fire at Bradford ground on 11 May which kills 40 fans.

7 July 1985. An unseeded 17-year-old, Boris Becker, wins Wimbledon men's singles.

28 Jan 1986. The American space shuttle Challenger explodes seconds after takeoff. Crew of seven perishes in spectacular blast.

15 April 1986. US aircraft, some flying from British bases, attack terrorist targets in Libya.

30 April 1986. A Russian nuclear reactor at Chernobyl is ablaze and is spewing radioactivity into the atmosphere.

6 March 1987. The British car ferry Spirit of Free Enterprise capsizes off Zeebrugge. Two hundred are feared dead.

16 Oct 1987. The "storm of the century" batters southern England causing enormous damage.

19 Oct 1987. Fifty billion pounds is wiped off value of public companies as bottom falls out of market in worst day for shares this century.

10 March 1988. Prince of Wales narrowly escapes death in avalanche near Klosters.

22 Dec 1988. Terrorist bomb sends Pan American jumbo jet crashing onto Scottish village of Lockerbie killing 259 passengers and at least 11 people on the ground.

9 June 1989. Chinese army opens fire on student dissidents in Peking's Tiananmen Square, killing several hundred. World reacts strongly.

3 Dec 1989. Mikhail Gorbachev and George Bush declare an end to the Cold War in Malta summit. Communism starts to collapse throughout Europe.

The Queen Mother's great-grandson is christened Prince William

London, 4 August 1982
The baby who is second in line to the throne was christened William Arthur Philip Louis in the music room at Buckingham Palace today. He was dressed in the well-used robe of cream satin and Honiton lace first used at the christenings of Queen Victoria's children and he behaved impeccably throughout the ceremony conducted by the Archbishop of Canterbury. Four generations of the royal family were present: Queen Elizabeth, the Queen Mother, Queen Elizabeth and Prince Philip, the Prince and Princess of Wales and the baby who, in the normal course of events, will become King William V. Born at St Mary's hospital, Paddington, on 21 June, he weighed 7lb 10ozs and had, according to the proud father, "a wisp of fair hair, sort of blondish, and blue eyes." The queen's reaction when she saw him was: "Thank goodness he hasn't got ears like his father." Both parents obviously dote on him, as do his grandparents and great-

Four generations of the royal family gather at the Palace for the christening.

grandmother, but there is concern in the royal family about Diana. She is suffering from post-natal depression and has become very thin. It is rumoured she has anorexia nervosa, the compulsive slimmer's disease, or bulimia, the nervous disorder whose victims gorge and are then sick. The obsession of the tabloid newspapers with "Lady Di" has become difficult for her to bear and the queen has asked editors to call off the professional photographers and allow her some privacy.

The fish take their revenge at last

London, 22 November 1982
The Queen Mother choked at a dinner party she was giving for friends tonight and was rushed to hospital where surgeons removed a fish bone from her throat. "After all these years of fishing," she says, "the fish are having their revenge."

Duchess of Windsor dies, sad and lonely

Paris, 24 April 1986
The Duchess of Windsor, who brought down a king and whose name filled front pages around the world, died a sad, lonely and almost forgotten woman at her home here today. In death, she will have her dearest wish: to lie alongside her husband, "dearest David" in the vault he had built for them at Windsor. The American divorcee, never accepted by the royal family in life, has joined them in death. She had been kept out of Britain by the Queen Mother's bitterness but even that had been softening. When the duchess wept at her husband's funeral, the Queen Mother took her arm and said: "I know how you feel. I've been through it myself."

Queen Mother leaving hospital.

The Duchess of Windsor for whose love King Edward gave up his throne.

A kiss for the bride: Andrew weds Fergie

Sprigs of shamrock for the Irish Guards

A new style: Prince Andrew and Sarah Ferguson play to crowd after wedding.

The Queen Mother surrounded by the Irish Guards on St Patrick's Day.

London, 23 July 1986
Prince Andrew married bubbly, red-haired Sarah Ferguson, daughter of Prince Charles's polo manager, in Westminster Abbey today. Just before the ceremony the queen created the bridegroom Duke of York, the title which formerly belonged to George VI, and Sarah is now Duchess of York. The bride wore a stunning dress by Linda Cierach which had an intertwined "S" and "A" motif. The crowds turned out, as usual, for the procession and cheered the newly-weds when they appeared, in high spirits, on the Buckingham Palace balcony where they gave each other an enthusiastic kiss – quite unlike the behaviour of the previous Duke and Duchess of York. They then left for their honeymoon cruise on *Britannia*.

London, 17 March 1987
Today is St Patrick's Day and the Queen Mother carried out one of the duties she looks forward to every year, the presentation of bunches of shamrock to the Irish Guards. They wear the green fronds in their caps and present her with a similar bunch to be pinned to her coat. She has carried on this tradition, begun by Queen Alexandra in 1901, since the early years of her marriage and takes obvious pleasure in having her photograph taken, a tiny smiling figure, surrounded by the big Irishmen, resplendent in their scarlet tunics. After the ceremony she enjoys a gin and tonic with the officers and then, as St Patrick's Day coincides with the climax of the National Hunt season, she either goes to the races or watches them on television.

Problems loom for royal family

London, 31 August 1989
Buckingham Palace announced today that the Princess Royal and Captain Mark Phillips have decided to separate after 15 years of marriage and two children. The announcement is especially painful to the Queen Mother who believes fiercely in the sanctity of marriage and grieved at Princess Margaret's troubles. Alas, this is only one of the problems looming for the royal family. Prince Charles and Diana are publicly demonstrating that the rumoured estrangement between them is fact rather than tabloid newspaper gossip. The Duke and Duchess of York's lifestyle is attracting criticism. And Prince Edward's abrupt resignation from the tough Royal Marines has not endeared him to traditionalists. In addition there is increasing political clamour for the queen, reputedly the richest woman in the world, to pay income tax just like her subjects.

The Queen Mother, wrapped up against the cold, walks with one of her corgis on the beach at Sandringham. She seems lonely, perhaps thinking of the days she walked there during her holidays with her beloved Bertie.

11 Feb 1990. President de Klerk lifts the ban on the African National Congress and promises to free Nelson Mandela.

31 March 1990. Huge anti-poll tax demonstration turns into a riot with hundreds of arrests.

2 August 1990. Iraq's massive army occupies Kuwait, sweeping aside all opposition.

3 Oct 1990. Bells peal out at midnight as Germany is reunited.

22 Nov 1990. After weeks of turmoil in Tory party Mrs Thatcher resigns leadership.

24 Feb 1991. In an offensive lasting just 100 hours Allied forces have crushed the Iraqi army and freed Kuwait.

21 May 1991. Prime Minister Rajiv Gandhi of India is killed near Madras by a suicide bomber, believed to be a woman Tamil dissident.

21 August 1991. The rush for freedom continues in eastern Europe as Mikhail Gorbachev returns to Moscow following collapse of coup against him.

26 October 1991. Dubrovnik, the "pearl of the Adriatic", is being battered by Serb artillery as the Serbs try to force the Croat defenders to surrender.

19 November 1991. Terry Waite, last of the British hostages held in Beirut, is freed after five years' captivity.

16 Sept 1992. Britain pulls out of the European exchange rate mechanism to allow the battered pound to float.

4 Nov 1992. Governor Bill Clinton of Arkansas unseats George Bush to become President of the US.

16 July 1993. Stella Rimington, head of MI5, holds a press conference "to dispel some of the more fanciful allegations" about her once-secret service.

13 Sept 1993. Yitzhak Rabin and Yassir Arafat shake hands on the lawn of the White House and sign agreement for limited Palestinian autonomy in Gaza and the West Bank.

4 Oct 1993. Yeltsin sends in tanks to shell parliament building and quell rebellion by hardliners in Moscow.

3 Dec 1993. Princess Diana reveals she is to withdraw from public life. Close to tears, she tells a charity lunch: "I hope you can find it in your hearts to understand and give me the time and space that has been lacking in recent years."

Happy 90th birthday, Queen Mum!

London, 4 August 1990
The Queen Mother is 90 today, the first queen in British history to reach that grand age. The celebrations started on June 28 with a parade in which she rode through London in an open carriage to a pageant in her honour on Horseguards Parade. The festivities continued on August 1 with a nostalgic tour of the East End streets she visited with the king during the Blitz fifty years ago. Members of the bombed-out families she comforted greeted her and she told them, "It's good to be back." Afterwards she boarded *Britannia* in the Pool of London for a family dinner and fireworks display. Today the crowds gathered as usual outside Clarence House to sing "Happy Birthday".

A courtly birthday kiss for the Queen Mother from a young admirer.

Controversial statue for 'Bomber' Harris

London, 31 May 1992
The Queen Mother unveiled a statue of Sir Arthur Harris, architect of the RAF's bombing of Germany, outside the RAF church of St Clement Danes in the Strand today. Ten demonstrators who called Harris a murderer and threw paint at the statue were arrested. The Queen Mother was unperturbed. "Sir Arthur," she said, "was an inspiring leader ... there was nowhere more fitting to honour him and his brave crews, more than 55,000 who died defending our country and freedom, than outside the RAF church."

Unveiling among the protests.

The second time round for Princess Anne

Balmoral, 12 December 1992
Today, the Princess Royal, better known locally as "wee Annie" married Commander Timothy Laurence, a career naval officer of Jewish descent, in the little stone church at Crathie. It was all a far cry from the pomp of Anne's first marriage to Captain Mark Phillips, a full state occasion in Westminster Abbey. This time, the princess and her new husband, attended by her children, Peter and Zara, exchanged vows in a simple ceremony. Everybody wore "ordinary" clothes and the only touch of pageantry was provided by two pipers. Neither Diana nor Sarah, estranged wives of her brothers, were there. The Queen Mother was there despite stories that she was so opposed to the remarriage of divorced members of her family that she would stay away. It seems that pressure from the queen and her love for her granddaughter prevailed.

Princess Anne and Commander Tim Laurence after their quiet wedding.

Windsor Castle blazes at end of disastrous year

London. 20 December 1992

There can be no doubt that this has been the worst year for the royal family since the abdication. At the Guildhall lunch to celebrate the 40th anniversary of her reign, the queen said that it has been an "Annus Horribilis". It has seen the divorce and remarriage of the Princess Royal, the separation of the Duke and Duchess of York, the publication of the notorious toe-sucking photographs of "Fergie" frolicking topless with her Texan "financial adviser", John Bryan, and the nightmarish end of the fairy tale marriage of Prince Charles and Diana in a blaze of public recrimination. On November 20 there was another disastrous blaze, when Windsor Castle, the only royal residence in continuous use since the Norman conquest, was severely damaged by a fire. It started when a spotlight set fire to a curtain in the private chapel, after a large picture

The destructive fire broke out just before noon and raged for seven hours.

A stunned Queen views the damage.

being stored in the chapel apparently pushed the curtain close to the spotlight. Flames leaped spectacularly into the sky, engulfing the State Apartments in the north-east corner of the Upper Quadrangle, destroy-ing most of the roof and weakening the structure. Most of the art treasures were rescued by the castle staff, led by the Duke of York, who passed paintings to safety by form-ing a human chain. But repairs to the fabric of the castle may cost as much as £60 million. It is small wonder that the queen in her Guildhall speech pleaded to be treated "with a touch of gentleness, good humour and understanding."

June 1992. Looking resplendent in Ceremonial Robes, the Queen Mother enjoys riding through the streets of Windsor on her way to the Order of the Garter Ceremony. Despite the pressures of the past few months, she is still smiling that sparkling smile and the crowds still flock to see her.

Armistice Day: the day she never forgets

London, 11 November 1993

Queen Elizabeth, the Queen Mother, joined veterans from both World Wars at the annual service of re-membrance and thanksgiving at Westminster Abbey today. This year marks the 75th anniversary of the Armistice which ended the carnage of World War I on the eleventh hour of the eleventh day of the eleventh month of 1918. The Queen Mother never misses the Armistice Day ser-vice or Sunday's commemoration when the old soldiers march past the Cenotaph, the sad notes of the Last Post echo along silent Whitehall and the nation remembers.

Dressed in black, her hat trimmed with white flowers and with two poppies pinned to her lapel, she arrived at the abbey to join the congre-gation of 2,000 in a service of hymns and readings. She stood with the others as Big Ben tolled the fateful hour and then laid a wreath on the tomb of the Unknown Warrior where she had laid her bridal bou-quet on her wedding day seventy years before. She then placed a cross in the Field of Remembrance in St Margaret's churchyard and, walking with the aid of a rolled umbrella, stopped to chat with the veterans.

She is one of them and this day is full of memories for her, of her brother, Fergus, killed in 1915, and of Gla-mis being turned into a military hospital; and she will never forget 1940 when she visited the smoulder-ing ruins of blitzed cities within hours of a raid and earned the grati-tude of the nation. She says, poi-gnantly, "we were all united then."

Queen Mother talks with old soldiers.

14 January 1994. Duchess of Kent is first member of royal family to become Roman Catholic in modern times.

26 January 1994. Student fires blank shots at Prince of Wales in Sydney, Australia.

16 March 1994. Bomb scare prevents Queen Mother presenting cup for race in her honour at Cheltenham.

6 May 1994. Queen Elizabeth and President Mitterrand open the Channel Tunnel.

23 June 1994. Government decides to decommission royal yacht *Britannia*.

6 August 1994. Mo Mowlam, the Labour Party's shadow National Heritage Secretary, unveils plans for Buckingham Palace and Windsor Castle to be sold off to a body such as the National Trust and for the royal family to be moved into a modern "People's Palace".

20 October 1994. Queen Elizabeth makes historic visit to Russia.

23 November 1994. Queen Mother attends thanksgiving service for diamond jubilee of Queen Elizabeth's Foundation for Disabled People.

10 January 1995. Camilla Parker-Bowles, the "other woman" in the marriage of the Prince and Princess of Wales, is to be divorced.

19 June 1995 Queen Elizabeth instals Lady Thatcher into the Order of the Garter, the highest decoration in her gift.

20 July 1995. Queen Mother is recovering well from a cataract operation.

4 August 1995. Queen Mother celebrates her 95th birthday with walkabout outside Clarence House.

28 September 1995. England's rugby captain, Will Carling, and his wife are to separate. His "close friendship" with Princess Diana is blamed.

10 November 1995. Queen Mother attends Remembrance Day service walking with the aid of two sticks. She goes ride-about among the veterans on her golf buggy.

3 December 1995. Princess Diana tells the *News of the World* that she often slips out at night to comfort the dying in London hospitals.

20 December 1995. Buckingham Palace announces that the Queen has told the Prince and Princess of Wales that in her view an early divorce is desirable.

Prince Charles: Grandmother is

Record 400 winners for Queen Mother

Nearco Bay leads the Queen Mother's string of horses at exercise.

Uttoxeter, 13 May 1994
Nearco Bay, a New Zealand bred 10-year-old, beat off a late challenge, "running like a hero" to win the Neville Lumb Silver Jubilee Handicap Chase here today and give the Queen Mother her 400th National Hunt winner. It is a record unsurpassed in steeple-chase history. She has been a most loyal supporter of the sport since the late Lord Mildmay persuaded her and her daughter, then Princess Elizabeth, to buy a jumper, Monaveen, which won for them in 1949. Monaveen's sad death in a race turned the princess from jumping to the flat but the Queen Mother has always accepted the uncertainties of steeplechasing along with its thrills. Three months ago Major Oliver Elwood, due to go to Bosnia with the Light Dragoons, was allowed by the army to delay his departure in order to ride her horse Keep Talking in the Grand Military Cup. They were both out of luck. The horse threw him. She chalked up another loser, but commiserated with him, and he went to Bosnia, bruised but comforted.

Racing certainty

At the Derby with Princess Anne.

Epsom, 1 June 1994
The one day of flat racing that the Queen Mother never misses is Derby Day, when Londoners flock to Epsom to enjoy the carnival atmosphere of the fun-fair, tipsters and the open-air picnics. Almost everybody in the country seems to have a bet on the Derby and the Queen Mother is no exception, although her bets are discreetly placed by a courtier. Win or lose, she cheers the horses home. Today, in the 215th running of the race, she watched Willie Carson win on Erhaab.

Queen Mother loses her oldest friend

London, 21 March 1994
Lady Hambleden, the last of the old guard in the Queen Mother's service, has died at 89. Patricia Hambleden will be sorely missed for she had been Lady-in-Waiting for 57 years and, as late as last June, accompanied the Queen Mother when she unveiled a statue to General de Gaulle in Carlton Gardens. Lady Hambleden was a member of the Herbert family which has served the royal household since Tudor times. Despite this royal linkage she was a down to earth character, a magistrate involved in local events, and was of particular value because she kept the Queen Mother in touch with life outside the royal circle.

Portsmouth, 5 June 1994. The royal yacht Britannia sails for Normandy to mark the 50th anniversary of D-Day. The Queen Mother stayed ashore but took part in the commemoration service with veterans of the landings.

'completely indefatigable and unstoppable'

Golden anniversary for the old soldiers

On parade: the Queen Mother steps out at the home of the Chelsea Pensioners.

Chelsea, 30 June 1994
The Queen Mother attended a drumhead service at the Royal Hospital, home of the "Chelsea Pensioners", today. The service was held to mark the 50th anniversary of the Army Benevolent Fund and to publicise its work. The fund was set up while the fighting in Normandy was raging and it was realised that there was no central military charity to care for soldiers and their families in need after the war. It has always been of special interest to the Queen Mother and the army returned that interest today with a pageant of military colour. Eight field marshals accompanied her and for the first time, the colours of every regiment in the army were on parade.

London, 14 July 1994. The Queen Mother attends the wedding of her granddaughter, Lady Sarah Armstrong-Jones, to artist Daniel Chatto at St Stephen's, Walbrook, and later she and Prince Charles host a reception for the newly-weds at Clarence House.

South Africa rejoins the Commonwealth

London, 20 July 1994
The Queen Mother attended a rousing service at Westminster Abbey today to welcome South Africa back into the Commonwealth after 33 years in the wilderness. Archbishop Tutu of Cape Town, in his customary ebullient form, told the congregation, "Like the prodigal son, South Africa is returning home and getting a right royal welcome. One can only say, Wow!" Bishop Trevor Huddleston, the veteran campaigner against apartheid, led the prayers of thanksgiving, the Elite Swingsters of Soweto performed the *Peace Song for South Africa*, and the congregation of 1,800 joined the choir in singing the Afrikaans and Zulu national anthems. After the service Queen Elizabeth and the Prince of Wales celebrated the occasion with a garden party in the grounds of Marlborough House.

Another glorious year for the Queen Mum

Birthday bouquet from an admirer.

London, 4 August 1994
Earlier this year Prince Charles, visiting New Zealand, said of his grandmother, "she is completely indefatigable and unstoppable... one of the most wonderful and remarkable people in the world". Today, on her 94th birthday, she went on a walkabout for three-quarters of an hour to greet the thousands of well-wishers who had gathered outside Clarence House. She looked frail and leaned on a stick but, seeing there were more people waiting in The Mall, she greeted them as well and nothing could detract from that famous smile as policemen ushered delighted children up to her to give her cards, flowers and balloons. Some people, regulars at these events, had camped out all night to be sure of a good place. She told them, "It's wonderful to see you all here". Eric Dunnington, a fire-eater, presented her with his customary birthday cake covered in peach and orange icing. Some red-coated toastmasters gave her champagne in a plastic cup. "Don't mind about the cup," she said, "I'm thirsty", and took a sip. Everybody joined in the singing of *Happy Birthday To You*, played by the Corps of Drums of the Grenadier Guards as gun salutes boomed out from Hyde Park and the Tower of London. The public celebrations over, she lunched with her family, then flew to Scotland to start her summer holiday at the Castle of Mey.

Queen Mother injures her leg in Scotland

London, 10 November 1994
An ankle injury sustained while the Queen Mother was on holiday in Scotland has forced her, most reluctantly, to cancel her Remembrance Day engagements. Officials at Buckingham Palace said today that the injury was not serious but that in a lady of her age even superficial injuries take a long time to heal. Meanwhile, her right ankle is heavily bandaged. This is the second time this year she has been forced to cancel her engagements. In January she had a chest infection which took a long time to clear. She suffers from arthritis and it has also been noticed that her eyesight is becoming blurred by cataracts. Old age is taking its toll – even of her.

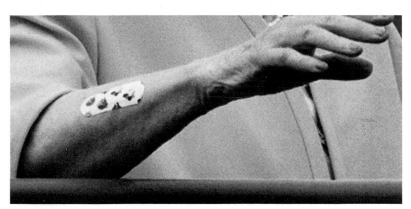

A Mickey Mouse plaster makes light of an injury to her arm.

The Queen Mother remembers the desperate

Queen pays tribute to a brave nation

London, 5 May 1995

The commemoration of the 50th anniversary of VE Day began today with an occasion of solemn pageantry when some 2,000 members of both Houses of Parliament, veterans and their families gathered in historic Westminster Hall, which survived a German incendiary bomb in 1941, to hear a formal address by the queen. Many were in tears and the Queen Mother was visibly moved when her daughter said: "Together we thank God for the victorious end to that titanic struggle of fifty years ago ... I remember my father and mother telling us at home of the courage and unity of purpose they encountered on all sides during their wartime travels and of the overwhelming sense that we were all united in a common resolve. These memories have remained with me all my life." Both the Speaker of the House of Commons, Betty Boothroyd, and the Lord Chancellor paid tribute to the example of King George VI and Queen Elizabeth the Queen Mother who "shared with their people the dangers through which they lived."

Shamrock date for the Irish Guards

London, 17 March 1995

It is St Patrick's Day and, as she had done for almost 70 years, the Queen Mother distributed fronds of shamrock, specially flown from Ireland, to the Irish Guards on parade at Chelsea Barracks. The men, with the shamrock in their cap bands, towered over her tiny, increasingly frail figure, but she obviously enjoyed every moment of the ceremony and it was carried out with an easy familiarity. It was noted, however, that this year for the first time, the queen also took part. Both the royal ladies wore huge bunches of the bright green shamrock on their coats and carried bouquets presented by the guardsmen.

Queen Mother is visibly moved as her daughter speaks in Westminster Hall.

Handshakes for heroes, holders of the Victoria Cross and George Cross.

The people salute their Queen Mum

London, 8 May 1995

The Queen Mother stepped out onto the balcony of Buckingham Palace today to a huge roar from a crowd which stretched half a mile down The Mall. With her daughters she was re-enacting one of the great scenes of British history when, with her beloved "Bertie" and Winston Churchill, they acknowledged the cheers of the crowd which had gathered outside the palace to celebrate the end of the war. Now they were celebrating the 50th anniversary of that day, VE Day.

She inaugurated the celebrations two days ago at a gathering in Hyde Park of 20,000 bemedalled veterans. Many, like her, walked with the aid of a stick, but they all held themselves proudly as she told them: "The day will bring back many memories and I do hope all of you will remember with pride and gratitude those men and women, armed and unarmed, whose courage really brought us to victory."

Yesterday she attended the service of thanksgiving, reconciliation and hope in St Paul's Cathedral and then helped entertain 56 visiting heads of state at lunch. Now, after two days of solemn memorial, the nation has let its hair down. Dame Vera Lynn sang *The White Cliffs of Dover* for the flag-waving crowd outside the palace, wartime aircraft flew down Pall Mall, and dazzling fireworks exploded over the palace. Everything went quiet when two minutes silence to honour the dead was observed but when the bugles sounded, the bonfires were lit and the parties went on into the night.

The day has truly belonged to the "Queen Mum". She is recognised as the last living symbol of the nation's fortitude during the years of danger and hardship. Now in her golden twilight, she can look on these celebrations as the culmination of a lifetime of duty. Never queen in her own right, her influence on her husband, her daughter and the nation has made her as important in this century as Queen Victoria was in the last. She has indeed been the nation's Queen Mother.

days of wartime sacrifice, courage and victory

The culmination of a lifetime of duty: the Queen Mother stars again in that famous balcony scene before a cheering audience at Buckingham Palace.

That joyous moment on the same balcony fifty years ago with the King and Winston Churchill waving to the crowd

19 June, 1995. Group Captain Peter Townsend died today at his home just outside Paris. He was 80. His death inevitably recalls his doomed romance with Princess Margaret but he had made a new life since then with his Belgian second wife, Marie Luce, and their three children. He lived in honourable exile as a writer in France and was regarded by his neighbours as the epitome of the English officer and gentleman.

Diana confesses to adultery on TV

London, 20 November 1995
Princess Diana gave an astonishing performance in a *Panorama* interview on the BBC tonight, admitting that she had slept with former Life Guards officer James Hewitt. Brimming with emotion, she told the stunned nation: "Yes, I adored him, yes, I was in love with him". She added that she was "absolutely devastated" when he wrote about their affair in a book. It was her night for revenge, expressing her doubts about her estranged husband's fitness to be king. She wants the crown to pass directly to her elder son, Prince William. As for herself, "I would like to be a queen in people's hearts...someone's got to go out there and love people and show it".

A 'tough old bird' gets a new hip

Queen Mother leaves hospital.

London, 4 December 1995
The Queen Mother, renowned in the royal family for being a "tough old bird", left the King Edward VII Hospital for Officers today less than three weeks after an operation to replace her right hip. At 95, she is one of the oldest patients to have undergone such surgery. She put on her usual professional show for the photographers. Impeccably dressed and wearing one of her trademark hats, she walked unaided except for two sticks, pausing to thank the hospital matron before being driven to Buckingham Palace. She is determined to continue to lead a busy life.

1996 - 2000

17 January 1996. Queen refuses to help the high-spending Duchess of York pay off her debts, estimated at £3 million.

17 April 1996. Duke and Duchess of York are granted a "quickie" divorce; she says they remain "the bestest of friends".

22 April 1996. Princess Diana causes furore when she is filmed standing by the operating table during open-heart surgery on seven-year-old boy.

5 December 1996. The Duchess of Kent is suffering from chronic fatigue syndrome, commonly known as ME.

1 May 1997. General Election brings the Labour Party under Tony Blair to power after 18 years of Conservative rule; with 418 seats against the Conservatives' 165, Labour has its largest-ever majority.

30 June 1997. Under a weeping monsoon sky, the Prince of Wales represents the Queen at the transfer of Hong Kong to the People's Republic of China after 156 years of British rule.

July 1997. Princess Diana meets Dodi Fayed on board his father's yacht while Prince Charles hosts Camilla Parker-Bowles' 50th birthday celebration at Highgrove.

4 August 1997. Queen Mother is 97 and she has her usual street party with well-wishers outside Clarence House; Prince William and Prince Harry are there, but the divorced Diana and Fergie are not.

11 November 1997. Queen Mother attends a special performance of Walt Disney's *Beauty and the Beast* in aid of the Entertainment Artistes' Benevolent Fund.

12 December 1997. The royal family paid an emotional farewell to their yacht *Britannia* at Portsmouth today when she was decommissioned after nearly 44 years of royal service.

2 February 1998. Queen Mother, recovering from her operation, is delighted to learn that her mare, Brand, which she was visiting when she broke her hip, has given birth to a foal.

19 March 1998. Queen Mother, walking with the aid of two sticks, is cheered as she presents the cup to the winner of the Queen Mother Champion Chase at Cheltenham.

24 March 1998. Prince William, on a skiing holiday in Canada with his father and brother, is given a pop-star welcome by adoring girls in Vancouver; one calls him "the king of babes".

Queen Mother pays tribute to war agents

At Westminster Abbey, honouring the heroes who "set Europe alight".

London, 13 February 1996
In her first public engagement since her hip operation the Queen Mother went to Westminster Abbey today to unveil a plaque in memory of the Allied agents who died behind enemy lines in World War II. She is patron of the Special Forces Club and takes a keen interest in the men and women of the Special Operations Executive, formed by Winston Churchill to "set Europe alight". Some 200 survivors of SOE watched as she drew the Union flag from the stone commemorating the 761 volunteers who gave their lives.

Vintage 96 and maturing well

Sandringham, 4 August 1996
The Queen Mother, who has spent her 96th birthday weekend at Sandringham, thanked well-wishers after church this morning, driving among them in her golf buggy which is shortly to be painted in her racing colours of old gold and light blue. Tomorrow, when she returns to Clarence House, her fans will greet her with champagne and flowers.

She travels now in her golf buggy.

Fairy-tale marriage comes to a sad end

London, 28 August 1996
The marriage of Charles and Diana, described on their wedding day by the Archbishop of Canterbury as "the stuff of which fairy tales are made", ended today in vengeful bitterness after months of hard-fought negotiation. The battle has not been pretty; it has been fought through "friends" in the press, television and books as the warring couple sought to gather public support. Intimate details have been disclosed in bugged telephone calls. Their affairs have become public property. Nobody has emerged clean and the only certain result is that the monarchy has been sorely damaged. Now, a civil servant's stamp has put an end to the 15-year marriage. Under the settlement Diana is to receive a lump-sum payment of £17 million, and will live in Kensington Palace with offices in St James's Palace; but the woman once seemingly destined to be queen has been stripped of the title of "Her Royal Highness". She will now be known officially as "Diana, Princess of Wales".

Normal service is resumed by the Queen Mother

London, 1997

The Queen Mother is having a busy year. She has fully recovered from her hip operation, her leg ulcer has healed and, despite her private anguish at the all-too-public break-up of the marriages of her grandsons Charles and Andrew, she is going about her duties with her customary steely determination. In February she positively glittered in a silver dress and diamonds at a Buckingham Palace banquet for President Weizman of Israel. Then, in May, she attended one of her favourite functions, the annual service at the Cavalry Memorial in Hyde Park, where she was surrounded by military horsemen. The following month she opened the restored East Market at the Smithfield meat market. She has had a long association with the market and is an expert judge and breeder of cattle. It was also an opportunity for her to be among the Cockneys who never forget the way she and her husband withstood the perils of the "Blitz" with them. There, she was greeted by one of the Cockneys' own royal family, the "Pearly King", Roy York. Then, on 4 August, she celebrated her 97th birthday. The Royal Regiment of Wales, preceded by Taffy, the regimental goat, marched past Clarence House playing *Happy Birthday*. She went walkabout and then lunched with her children, grandchildren and great-grandchildren.

Glittering at a Buckingham Palace banquet given by the Queen for Israel's President Weizman on 25 February 1997.

21 May 1997. The Queen Mother among her soldiers. She attends the 73rd annual service at the Cavalry Memorial in London's Hyde Park.

11 June 1997. She opens the newly restored East Market at Smithfield meat market and meets one of London's traditional "Pearly Kings".

Princess Diana's death shocks the world

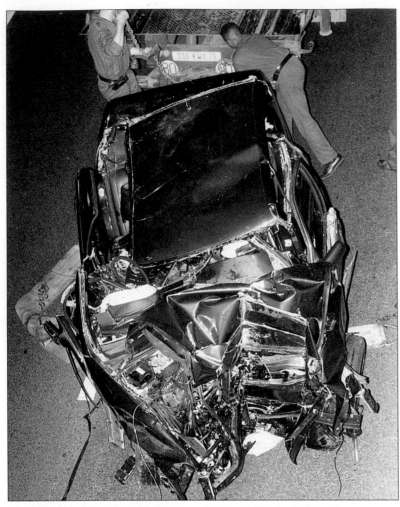

Mercedes is crushed by high-speed crash into a pillar in Paris underpass.

Wealthy Egyptian Dodi Fayed was the new love in divorced Princess's life.

Paris, 30 August 1997

Princess Diana died early this morning in an horrendous car crash in the Place de l'Alma underpass in Paris. Her new love, Dodi Fayed, son of Mohamed Fayed, owner of the Ritz in Paris and Harrods in London, died with her when their car smashed into a pillar in the tunnel at nearly 90 miles an hour. Their driver, Henri Paul, a member of the Ritz security staff, also died in the crash. Early reports say he had been drinking heavily. The only survivor is Dodi Fayed's bodyguard, Trevor Rees-Jones, who is badly injured. Diana and Dodi's romance began when they met on board his father's yacht *Jonikal* at St Tropez last month. Diana was blissfully happy and when they arrived in Paris last night after cruising off Sardinia there were expectations that they would announce their engagement. The paparazzi were waiting for them and chased the lovers around Paris. They took refuge in the Ritz restaurant, but left when the other diners stared at them. They fled with Henri Paul boasting to the photographers, "Don't bother to follow, you won't catch us". A few minutes later he and Dodi were dead. Diana was fatally injured. Her death has shocked the world. She is mourned with tears and anger.

Millions of flowers are sent by ordinary people mourning Diana's death. They carpet the pavement outside Westminster Abbey as the royal family arrive.

Diana's death shakes the Royals

Westminster, 6 Sept 1997

The public's discontent with the royal family's treatment of Princess Diana manifested itself in extraordinary fashion during her funeral service today. In his tribute speech her brother, Earl Spencer, promised Diana that her "blood family" would attempt to continue her "imaginative and loving" upbringing of her two sons, contrasted with the "duty and tradition" in which they might otherwise be immersed. His pledge amounted to a challenge to the royal family and, as its meaning was grasped by the thousands listening outside the Abbey, a wave of clapping began which rolled into the nave and was taken up inside by Diana's friends, while the Queen and her family sat stoney-faced. It summed up the way in which the Queen, obeying the strict rules of protocol, had been left far behind by her people, who had chosen to mourn the loss of their "Queen of Hearts" in the emotional way in which she had lived her life. The Queen has already responded to the popular mood, however. In a TV broadcast before the funeral, she paid moving tribute to Diana as an "exceptional and gifted human being", suggesting that the Queen will heed the lesson that the monarchy must adapt in order to survive.

A quiet wedding at Windsor

The newly titled Earl of Wessex and his bride pose for photographers on the steps of St George's Chapel.

Windsor, 19 June 1999

Prince Edward, the Queen's youngest son and seventh in line to the throne, married 34-year-old public relations executive Sophie Rhys-Jones in a 45-minute ceremony at Windsor this afternoon. The couple went out of their way to avoid the royal pomp and national celebrations associated with the ill-fated marriages of Edward's siblings. The ceremony was held at 5 p.m. in the relative intimacy of St George's Chapel, and an informal tone was set by asking guests not to wear hats. But the event was still watched by an estimated 200 million TV viewers worldwide. In a surprise announcement before the ceremony the Queen conferred the titles of Earl and Countess of Wessex on the couple, who have made it clear that they intend to live largely outside royal circles.

Queen Mother sprightly as she enters her hundredth year

Meeting birthday well-wishers.

London, 4 August 1999

The Queen Mother celebrated her 99th birthday in style today, belying concerns about the state of her health. She emerged from her London home, Clarence House, at 11.15 a.m., supported only by a walking stick, to be greeted by the crowd of well-wishers who had gathered outside. The Welsh Guards marched past, giving a stirring rendition of "Happy Birthday To You", after which the Queen Mother received gifts of cards, balloons, and flowers from children. She then walked across the road to talk to people in the crowd. She was on her feet for half an hour before taking to her golf buggy, which was decorated with balloons for the festive occasion.

The Queen Mother's birthday was completed by lunch with members of her family and a trip to the theatre in the evening. It was a remarkable performance for a person who has now undergone two hip replacement operations, the first in 1995 and the second in 1998. The Queen Mother was also admitted to hospital early this year after a series of severe nosebleeds. Yet she remains active and robust, regularly attending race meetings and events of particular personal significance for her, such as the Remembrance Day ceremony. The warmth and affection of the crowd's response to her birthday walkabout clearly reflects the Queen Mother's continuing popularity with the public at large.

Centenary begins at the Royal Mint

London, 10 January 2000

With seven months still to go before the Queen Mother's hundredth birthday, the Royal Mint today issued a commemorative £5 centenary coin. It shows the Queen Mother in profile, smiling graciously against a background of flag-waving crowds. The artist responsible for the portrait, Ian Rank-Broadley, said he wanted to show "Her Majesty's dignified bearing of many years, but retain the elegance and grace for which she is so admired." Planning is already well under way for a month of birthday celebrations, which will begin with a thanksgiving service at St Paul's cathedral on 11 July.

115

- Visiting Dartmouth, appears smitten by dashing Prince Philip 07/39
- Is made a Colonel of the Grenadier Guards 04/42
- Marks her entry into public life at 16. Takes the salute 04/42
- Would like to be a nurse or join ATS but the king says no 04/42
- Joins the ATS as officer cadet 03/45
- Joins the crowds in the streets celebrating VE Day 05/45
- Walks the Derby course with her mother 1947
- Makes 21st birthday broadcast to South Africans 04/47
- Becomes engaged to Prince Philip of Greece 07/47
- Marries Prince Philip at Westminster Abbey 11/47
- Gives birth to her first baby, Prince Charles 11/48
- Has a daughter, Anne, at Clarence House 08/50
- Hopes to go back to her life in Malta after Anne's birth 08/50
- Visits Canada and United States with the Duke 11/51
- Returns to England as Queen Elizabeth II 02/52
- Churchill meets her at Heathrow to pay homage 02/52
- Millions watch her coronation at home on television 06/53
- Asks Margaret to wait 2 years before marrying Peter Townsend 06/53
- Annigoni's portrait breaks attendance records at the Royal Academy 08/55
- Attacked as "priggish" by Lord Altrincham in a magazine 08/57
- The last debutantes are presented at Court 03/58
- Gives birth to a second son, Andrew, future Duke of York 02/60
- Gives birth to a third son, Prince Edward 03/64
- Takes Trooping the Colour then shows Edward to the people 06/64
- Invests her son Charles as Prince of Wales 07/69
- A year of Jubilee tours of her country and Commonwealth 1977
- The whole nation shares her Silver Jubilee celebrations 06/77
- Her son Charles marries Lady Diana Spencer 07/81
- Her son, Prince Andrew, fights in the Falkland conflict 06/82
- Problems loom with gossip about her children's private lives 08/89
- Political clamour for her to pay taxes 08/89
- In a speech says it has been an "Annus Horribilis" 12/92
- A garden party for South Africa's return to Commonwealth 07/94
- Makes a historic visit to Russia 10/94
- For the first time, goes with her mother to present shamrock 03/95
- Makes a moving VE-Day anniversary address to Parliament 05/95

- Tells Charles and Diana that divorce is desirable 12/95
- Refuses to help Duchess of York pay off her debts 01/96
- Receives President Weizman of Israel 02/97
- At Balmoral, hears of Princess Diana's death 08/97
- Faces nation's disquiet as she obeys the mourning protocol 09/97
- On TV, pays tribute to Diana 09/97
- On her golden wedding, responds to the public's criticism 11/97
- Emotional farewell to the "Britannia" 12/97

Elizabeth, Princess future Queen Elizabeth II
- See: Elizabeth II, Queen

Elizabeth, Queen The Queen Mother
- Born at her family's London home, 17, Bruton Street 08/00
- Her 10th birthday is typical of her happy childhood 08/10
- Account of her first meeting with her future husband 08/10
- Comes out into Society as a debutante at Holyrood Palace 07/20
- Is bridesmaid to her friend Princess Mary 02/22
- Hesitates whilst "Bertie" is relentless in pursuit of her 04/22
- Her engagement to the Duke of York is announced 01/23
- With her parents, visits her prospective in-laws 01/23
- With her fiance, carries out her first duties, in Edinburgh 03/23
- Marries Albert at Westminster Abbey 04/23
- Becomes patron of YWCA and NSPCC 06/23
- First appearance as member of the royal family is at Hendon 06/23
- Stands as godmother to King Alexander of Serbia's son 10/23
- Charity events are a vital part of royal duty: pictures 1924
- Visit to Queen's University, Belfast, to unveil war memorial 07/24
- Back to royal duties after African tour 1925
- On tour in Africa with her husband, enjoys a safari 01/25
- Suffers for her husband as his speech is ruined by nerves 05/25
- At Glamis for the season, she hopes that she is pregnant 08/25
- Gives birth to Elizabeth Alexandra Mary at 17, Bruton Street 04/26
- She goes fishing at Lake Taupo 02/27
- Crossing the equator on HMS Renown 02/27
- New Zealand visit is huge success, but she misses her baby 03/27
- "The whole continent is in love with her" says governor 05/27
- The king makes her Colonel-in-Chief of King's Own Yorkshires 08/27
- To take over presentation of St Patrick's Day shamrock 08/27

- She has greatly impressed the king and he is spellbound 09/27
- Gives birth to a second daughter, Margaret Rose 08/30
- Visiting the Colonial Exhibition in Paris 07/31
- In Scotland for her parents' golden wedding 08/31
- Falls in love with The Royal Lodge, their new home 09/31
- Raises money for charity as economic crisis hits the nation 11/31
- Employs a governess, Marion Crawford 04/32
- At Fort Belvedere, meets Wallis Simpson 01/33
- Touring industrial areas, meets Welsh miners 04/33
- Concerned over the effects of the Prince of Wales's affair 12/34
- Proudly presents new colours to the Black Watch 08/35
- Develops pneumonia during Christmas at Sandringham 12/35
- Attends the funeral of King George V 01/36
- A bouquet for the duchess who has a passion for flowers 07/36
- Opens Infirmary instead of the king who goes to meet Wallis 09/36
- Refuses to speak to Mrs Simpson 09/36
- Furious with the king as the constitutional crisis deepens 12/36
- Fears for her family as abdication seems possible 12/36
- She becomes Queen Consort as "Bertie" becomes King George VI 12/36
- The first Scottish queen since Mary, Queen of Scots 12/36
- The State Coach carries king and queen to their coronation 05/37
- In a gown of ivory satin and gold thread, she is crowned 05/37
- Attends her first Remembrance Ceremony as queen 11/37
- Sees the king present new colours to the Grenadier Guards 05/38
- Receives the Order of the Thistle at the Empire Exhibition 05/38
- Sadness as her mother dies 06/38
- A State visit to Paris where her gowns are much admired 07/38
- Launches the liner Queen Elizabeth 09/38
- With Neville Chamberlain on the Palace balcony after Munich 09/38
- Takes Princess Elizabeth to see "Where the Rainbow Ends" 12/38
- Adamant that the Windsors not be allowed back 1939
- Joins the king in welcoming the French president to London 03/39
- On a State visit to Canada, winning many new friends 05/39

- She charms the Americans and takes New York by storm 06/39
- Huge cheering crowds welcome home their king and queen 06/39
- Hurries to the king's side as he faces the prospect of war 08/39
- Upon the declaration of war says "I must be with the king" 09/39
- Sets an example to the country with her palace work parties 09/39
- Broadcasts to the women of the empire on Armistice Day 11/39
- Tours the country meeting and encouraging the people 11/39
- Declines uniform so that people shall see her at her best 12/39
- Meets families of the men who died on Ajax and Exeter 02/40
- Becomes a "billeter" taking in royal refugees 05/40
- Intends to stay and fight 05/40
- Dismisses suggestions that the princesses be evacuated 06/40
- Has a revolver given to her by Churchill 06/40
- Narrowly escapes death when Buckingham Palace is bombed 09/40
- Can "now look East End in the face" after the Palace bomb 09/40
- Welcomes Canadian troops, come to help fight the war 1942
- Visits her old home, now housing the recovering wounded 1942
- Hears of the Duke of Kent's death in an aircrash 08/42
- Appointed Counsellor of State whilst king tours Middle-East 06/43
- Decorates Guy Gibson with VC 06/43
- Oversees Windsor Great Park farm in "Dig for Victory" drive 06/43
- Visits a USAAF base 08/43
- Much distressed by her father's death 11/44
- The war ends. Churchill has called her "that valiant woman" 04/45
- With her family, greets the joyful crowds from the balcony 05/45
- Goes with the king to join the East Enders in celebration 05/45
- Goes to meet the newly-liberated Channel Islanders 06/45
- Walks the Derby course with Princess Elizabeth 1947
- The South African tour is beset with problems 04/47
- Hits South African over the head, believing him an assassin 04/47
- Her daughter Princess Elizabeth marries 11/47
- Cheering crowds as she and the king drive through London 11/47
- She and the king speak to the nation on their anniversary 11/47

- Celebrates her silver wedding with the king and the nation 04/48
- Becomes a grandmother as Prince Charles is born 11/48
- Relieved at the king's recovery for Prince Charles' baptism 12/48
- A worrying time as the king undergoes surgery 03/49
- Will take on more duties as the king is ordered to rest 03/49
- Goes with the king to his favourite show, the Royal Variety 11/50
- Takes the sick king's place on a Festival visit to Cardiff 05/51
- With the king and Queen Mary, opens the Festival of Britain 05/51
- Her anxiety obvious as she goes alone to Royal Variety 11/51
- Spends a rare day off at Sandown Park with Princess Margaret 12/51
- Insists that the king pre-record his Christmas broadcast 12/51
- At Sandringham for Christmas, fears for her husband's health 12/51
- Comforts her husband as Elizabeth leaves on a royal tour 01/52
- Churchill praises her valour 02/52
- Distraught at the death of her beloved "Bertie" 02/52
- Remains at Sandringham where her husband lies in state 02/52
- Her beloved "Bertie" is laid to rest at Windsor 02/52
- Does not invite Duke of Windsor to the funeral lunch 02/52
- Wishes to be known as Queen Elizabeth, The Queen Mother 02/52
- In a message to the nation, commends her "dear daughter" 02/52
- Comforted by the whole world's sympathy at the king's death 02/52
- The needs of the Black Watch bring her back into public 05/52
- Watches proudly as her daughter is crowned 06/53
- Takes Princess Margaret on a tour of Rhodesia 06/53
- Another triumphant trip to North America 11/54
- Welcomed home from America by adoring crowds 11/54
- At her first ball since her husband's death 11/56
- Presents St David's Day leeks to the Welch Guards 03/57
- Sets out on a world tour 01/58
- Attends the wedding of her daughter, Princess Margaret 05/60
- Keeps up a non-stop round of work: pictures 1963
- Enjoys Trooping the Colour with her six grandchildren 06/64
- Her great friend, Mary, the Princess Royal dies 03/65
- Visiting Germany, goes to see the Commonwealth War Graves 07/65
- In Australasia, visits Prince Charles and goes fishing 04/66

Gustav, King of Sweden
- Offers to mediate with Hitler. King George refuses the offer 08/40

H

Haakon, King of Norway
- Arrives to take refuge in Buckingham Palace 05/40
- Godfather to his great-nephew Prince Charles 12/48

Hambledon, Lady Patricia
- The Queen Mother's friend and Lady-in-Waiting; dies aged 89 03/94

Hartnell, Norman
- Designs stunning gowns for the queen's State visit to Paris 07/38
- Creates Princess Elizabeth's bridal gown 11/47

Henry, Prince "Harry"
- Born at Paddington Hospital 09/84
- At Balmoral, hears of his mother's death 08/97
- Earl Spencer's pledge to his nephews at the funeral 09/97

Henry, Prince second son of Prince Charles and Diana
- See: Henry, Prince "Harry"

Henry, Prince son of George V
- See: Gloucester, Prince Henry, Duke of

Hong Kong
- Transferred to China after 156 years of British rule 06/97

Honolulu (Hawaii)
- The Queen Mother visits as part of her world tour 01/58

Huddleston Trevor, Bishop (anti-apartheid campaigner)
- Celebrates the return of South Africa to the Commonwealth 07/94

I – J – K

India
- Lord Mountbatten's plan for partition is agreed by Britain 05/47
- British rule ends after 163 years 08/47
- Proclaimed a republic 01/50

Irish Guards The
- Elizabeth to take over the St Patrick's Day shamrock duty 08/27
- For the first time, the queen comes to the shamrock ceremony 03/95

Juliana Princess of the Netherlands
- Arrives with her family to take refuge in Buckingham Palace 05/40

Kent, Katherine Duchess of
- Becomes a Roman Catholic 01/94
- Suffers from chronic fatigue syndrome (ME) 12/96

Kent, Prince Edward Duke of
- Becomes Duke of Kent upon his father's death in an aircraft 08/42

Kent, Prince George Duke of
- Ends visit to Canada with his brother the Prince of Wales 09/26
- Appointed Governor-General of Australia 10/38
- Killed as his plane crashes into a hill 08/42

Kent, Princess Marina Duchess of
- Marries Prince George, Duke of Kent at Westminster Abbey 11/34
- Death of her husband in aircrash 08/42

Kenya
- Princess Elizabeth is told of her father's death 02/52

King's Own Yorkshire Light Infantry
- Duchess of York becomes Colonel-in-Chief of the regiment 08/27

King, Mackenzie (Prime Minister of Canada)
- Talks with the king and Roosevelt into the night 06/39

L

Lang, Cosmo (Archbishop of Canterbury)
- Officiates at the wedding of Albert and Elizabeth 04/23
- Baptises Princess Elizabeth 05/26
- Conducts the historic coronation ceremony 05/37

Lascelles, Henry Viscount
- Marries Princess Mary, only daughter of the king 02/22

Laurence, Commander Timothy
- Becomes the second husband of the Princess Royal 12/92

Linley, David Viscount
- Born to Princess Margaret and Lord Snowdon 11/61

Logue, Lionel (speech therapist)
- Called in by the Duchess of York to help her husband 1927

London
- The capital prepares its defences as the fear of war grows 08/39
- King and queen visit blitzed areas almost every day 09/40
- Wild celebration for VE Day 05/45
- The people camp out to await the royal wedding procession 11/47
- The late king makes his last journey through the streets 02/52
- Millions line the streets for the coronation of Elizabeth 06/53
- The capital welcomes the Queen Mother home from America 11/54
- A huge display of love for the Queen on her Silver Jubilee 06/77
- VE Day anniversary climaxes at Buckingham Palace 05/95

Lyautey, Marshal (founder of modern Morocco)
- Guides the royals on their visit to the Colonial Exhibition 07/31

M

Malta
- The king relaxes during a gruelling tour of Middle East 06/43
- Princess Elizabeth enjoys normal life as a sailor's wife 08/50

Margaret, Princess Countess of Snowdon
- Born at Glamis Castle 08/30

- Out and about in London with "Crawfie" 07/35
- Welcomes her parents home from America 06/39
- Joins the crowds in the streets celebrating VE Day 05/45
- On tour with her parents in South Africa 04/47
- Courtiers anxious about her affection for Peter Townsend 04/47
- Godmother to her nephew Prince Charles 12/48
- A last dinner with her father before he dies in his sleep 02/52
- Her love for Peter Townsend becomes public knowledge 06/53
- A trip to Rhodesia aimed at separating her from Townsend 06/53
- Announces her decision to give up Peter Townsend 10/55
- Marries Antony Armstrong-Jones at Westminster Abbey 05/60
- Gives birth to a son, David, Viscount Linley 11/61
- Gives birth to a daughter, Lady Sarah Armstrong-Jones 05/64
- Separates from Lord Snowdon after 15 years of marriage 03/76

Marina, Princess of Greece
- See: Kent, Princess Marina, Duchess of

Mary, Queen wife of George V
- Attends, with the king, memorial service for Tsar 07/18
- Has been to Glamis to inspect Elizabeth and approves 09/21
- Receives her future daughter-in-law and her parents 01/23
- Stands as godmother to her granddaughter Princess Elizabeth 05/26
- The nation celebrates the king's Silver Jubilee 05/35
- Her husband dead, she kisses the hand of Edward in homage 01/36
- Urges Edward to put his duty to his country first 11/36
- Refuses Edward's request that she receive Mrs Simpson 11/36
- Imperious as her son Edward leaves after abdicating 12/36
- Breaks with tradition by attending the coronation 05/37
- Godmother to her great-grandson Prince Charles 12/48
- Kisses the hand of her granddaughter the new Queen Elizabeth 02/52
- The indomitable widow of King George V dies 03/53

Mary, The Princess Royal
- Marries Henry, Viscount Lascelles. Elizabeth is bridesmaid 02/22
- Stands as godmother to her niece Princess Elizabeth 05/26
- Weeps as her brother Edward leaves after abdicating 12/36
- Sees her brother present new colours to the Grenadier Guards 05/38
- Dies, aged 67, at Harewood Castle 03/65

Mary, The Princess Royal daughter of George V

- Makes friends with Lady Elizabeth through the Girl Guides 09/19

Mey, Castle of
- The Queen Mother buys this home as a Scottish hideaway 06/53
- The Queen Mother, on her 94th birthday, comes for a holiday 08/94

Michael, Prince of Kent
- Son of Prince George, Duke of Kent 08/42

Milford Haven, Victoria Dowager Marchioness of
- Godmother to her great-grandson Prince Charles 12/48

Mitterrand, Francois President (of France)
- Welcomes the Queen Mother on her visit to Paris 1982

Montgomery Field Marshal Lord
- Defeats Rommel at El Alamein 10/42

Mountbatten Lord Louis
- Becomes Supreme Allied Commander South-East Asia 08/43
- His plans for his nephew fulfilled with the royal engagement 07/45
- Cabinet agrees his plan for the partition of India 05/47
- Presides over the dissolution of the Indian Raj 08/47
- Is assassinated by the IRA whilst on holiday in Ireland 08/79

Mowlam, Mo (Labour MP)
- Says the royal family should live in a "People's Palace" 08/94

N – O – P

Nearco Bay (racehorse)
- Is the Queen Mother's record 400th National Hunt winner 05/94

New Zealand
- Gives a tumultuous welcome to its royal visitors 03/27
- The Queen Mother is welcomed back by enthusiastic crowds 02/58
- The Queen Mother goes fishing here again 04/66

Nicholas Tsar of Russia
- Abdicates 03/17
- Murdered, with his family, by Bolsheviks. Memorial Service 07/18

Olav Crown Prince of Norway
- Arrives to take refuge in Buckingham Palace 05/40

Paris
- The State visit by King George VI and his queen is a triumph 07/38
- Churchill arrives in an attempt to boost French morale 05/40
- Princess Diana and Dodi Fayed die in a car crash 08/97

Parker-Bowles, Camilla
- Is to divorce Brigadier Andrew Parker-Bowles 01/95
- Prince Charles hosts her 50th birthday celebration 07/97

Philip, Prince of Greece
- See: Edinburgh, Prince Philip, Duke of

Phillips, Captain Mark
- Marries Princess Anne at Westminster Abbey 11/73

- His separation from Princess Anne is announced 08/89

Phillips, Peter
- Son of Princess Anne and Mark Phillips, born 15 November '77
- Attends the marriage of his mother to Timothy Laurence 12/92

Phillips, Zara
- Daughter of Princess Anne and Mark Phillips, born 15 May '81
- Attends the marriage of her mother to Timothy Laurence 12/92

Q – R

Queen Elizabeth (ocean liner)
- The queen launches her namesake on Clydebank 09/38
- Makes secret maiden voyage to New York 03/40

Queen Elizabeth's Foundation for Disabled People
- The Queen Mother attends its Diamond Jubilee thanksgiving 11/94

Rees-Jones, Trevor (Dodi Fayed's bodyguard)
- Only survivor after the crash in which Diana and Dodi died 08/97

Renown, HMS
- Takes the royal couple to Australasia 02/27

Rhys-Jones, Sophie
- Marries Prince Edward 06/99

Roosevelt, Franklin Delano President (USA)
- The royal couple stay with him for their last night in US 06/39
- Meets Churchill at sea and proclaims the Atlantic Charter 08/41
- Inaugurated for a fourth term in office 01/45
- Dies suddenly, aged 63 04/45

Roosevelt, Mrs Eleanor
- Meets the queen during the State visit to the United States 06/39
- Visiting England, experiences its wartime hardships 11/42

Rothermere, Lord
- Colludes with Beaverbrook to hush up scandal about the king 08/36
- Lifts the gag on the press; now the country knows 12/36

Royal Hospital home of the Chelsea Pensioners
- The Queen Mother at Army Benevolent Fund's 50th anniversary 06/94

Royal Lodge Windsor Great Park
- To be the new home of the Yorks 09/31
- A happy home for the Yorks, their daughters and many pets 07/36

Russia
- The queen makes a historic visit 10/94

S

Sandown Park (racecourse)
- The queen and Princess Margaret spend a day at the races 12/51

Sandringham
- The king and queen receive Elizabeth and her family 01/23

- The royal family gather for a traditional Christmas 12/51
- The king arrives after saying goodbye to his daughter 02/52
- The king dies in his sleep, only 56 years of age 02/52
- King George VI lies in state 02/52

Simpson, Mrs Wallis
- See: Windsor, Wallis, Duchess of

Snowdon, Antony Earl of
- Marries Princess Margaret at Westminster Abbey 05/60
- Princess Margaret gives birth to son, David, Viscount Linley 11/61
- His daughter Lady Sarah Armstrong-Jones is born 05/64
- Separates from Princess Margaret after 15 years of marriage 03/76

South Africa
- A royal tour is proving less than successful 04/47
- Is welcomed back into the Commonwealth 07/94

Spencer, Charles Earl
- His sister, Diana, dies in a car crash in Paris 08/97
- His tribute to Diana affects the royal family 09/97

Spencer, John Earl
- Gives his daughter, Diana, in marriage to Prince Charles 07/81

Spencer, Lady Diana
- See: Wales, Diana, The Princess of

St Paul's Cathedral
- King George V and Queen Mary celebrate the Silver Jubilee 05/35
- A special service to celebrate the royal silver wedding 04/48
- A thanksgiving service for the Queen' Silver Jubilee 06/77
- The Prince of Wales marries Lady Diana Spencer 07/81

St Paul's Walden Bury
- In the garden, Elizabeth accepts "Bertie's" third proposal 01/23
- Now a convalescent home for the wounded 1942

Strathmore, Cecilia Countess of
- Gives birth to Lady Elizabeth Bowes Lyon 08/00
- With her husband and daughter, visits the king and queen 01/23
- Her daughter, Elizabeth, marries the Duke of York 04/23
- Stands as godmother to her granddaughter Princess Elizabeth 05/26
- Golden wedding celebrations at Glamis 08/31
- Dies, after a long illness, aged 75 06/38

Strathmore, Claude Earl of
- Father of Lady Elizabeth Bowes Lyon 08/00
- With his wife and daughter, visits the king and queen 01/23
- His daughter, Elizabeth, marries the Duke of York 04/23
- Golden wedding celebrations at Glamis 08/31
- Dies, aged 89, at Glamis 11/44

——————— T ———————

Tasmania
- Galeforce winds can't dampen the welcome for the "Queen Mum" 02/58

Thatcher, Margaret
- Becomes Britain's first woman prime minister 05/79
- Resigns as prime minister 11/90
- The queen instals her into the Order of the Garter 06/95

Townsend, Peter
- Accompanies the royal family on its South African tour 04/47
- Courtiers are concerned over Princess Margaret's interest 04/47
- His affair with Princess Margaret is public knowledge 06/53
- Princess Margaret decides to give him up 10/55
- Dies, aged 80 06/95

Tutu, Desmond Archbishop of Capetown
- Celebrates the return of South Africa to the Commonwealth 07/94

——————— U – V – W ———————

Victoria and Albert The Royal Yacht
- On a cruise, Princess Elizabeth meets Prince Philip 07/39

Victoria, Queen
- Dies, aged 81 01/01
- Buried at Windsor Castle 02/01

Wales, Charles, The Prince of
- Born 14 November, baptised Charles Philip Arthur George 12/48
- His sister, Princess Anne is born 08/50
- Attends his mother's coronation 06/53
- Invested as Prince of Wales at Caernarfon Castle 07/69
- Marries Lady Diana Spencer at St Paul's Cathedral 07/81
- His wife gives him a son, to be named William 06/82
- His second son, Henry, to be called "Harry" is born 09/84
- Narrowly escapes death in an avalanche whilst skiing 03/88
- Separates from his wife 1991
- Says that his grandmother is "unstoppable" 1994
- Blank shots fired at him in Sydney, Australia 01/94
- With the Queen Mother, hosts Lady Sarah's wedding reception 07/94
- Princess Diana confesses to adultery on the BBC 11/95
- The queen tells him that divorce is desirable 12/95
- Divorces Princess Diana 08/96
- Represents the Queen at the tranfer of Hong Kong to China 06/97
- Hosts Camilla Parker-Bowles' 50th birthday celebration 07/97
- At Balmoral, hears of Princess Diana's death 08/97
- Affected by Earl Spencer's tribute to Diana 09/97

Wales, Diana, The Princess of
- Marries the Prince of Wales at St Paul's Cathedral 07/81

- Gives birth to a son, William Arthur Philip Louis 06/82
- Concern over her health 08/82
- Her second son, Henry, to be called "Harry" is born 09/84
- Her estrangement from her husband is obvious in public 08/89
- Separates from her husband 1991
- Confesses to adultery on the BBC 11/95
- The queen tells her that divorce is desirable 12/95
- Causes anger when filmed at an open-heart surgery on a child 04/96
- Divorces Prince Charles 08/96
- Meets Dodi Fayed at St Tropez 07/97
- Dies with Dodi in a car crash in Paris 08/97
- People mourn her death all over the world 08/97
- The Union flag is flown at half-mast in her memory 09/97
- A state funeral for the "Queen of Hearts" 09/97

Wales, Edward, The Prince of son of George V
- See: Windsor, Prince Edward, Duke of

Welch Guards
- The Queen Mother presents the St David's Day leeks as usual 03/57

Westminster Abbey
- Coronation of Edward VII 08/02
- Scene of the glittering wedding of Albert and Elizabeth 04/23
- The wedding of the Duke of Kent to Princess Marina of Greece 11/34
- Trumpets sound, bells peal, as King George VI is crowned 05/37
- Princess Elizabeth marries Prince Philip 11/47
- Queen Elizabeth II is crowned 06/53
- Princess Margaret marries Antony Armstrong-Jones 05/60
- Princess Anne marries Captain Mark Phillips 11/73
- Prince Andrew marries Sarah Ferguson 07/86
- A state funeral for Princess Diana 09/97

William, Prince
- Born to Charles and Diana, the Prince and Princess of Wales 06/82
- Is christened at Buckingham Palace 08/82
- Princess Diana wants the crown to pass directly to him 11/95
- At Balmoral, hears of his mother's death 08/97
- Earl Spencer's pledge to his nephews at the funeral 09/97
- Called the "king of babes" by adoring Canadian girls 03/98

William, Prince first son of Charles, Prince of Wales
- See: William, Prince

Windsor Castle
- Queen Victoria is buried beside Albert 02/01
- King George V is buried in St Georges Chapel 01/36
- Queen oversees Windsor Great Park "Dig for Victory" farm 06/43
- King George VI is buried 02/52

- The queen lights the first Jubilee beacon 06/77
- Severely damaged in a fire 11/92

Windsor, Prince Edward Duke of
- Investiture at 17, as Prince of Wales 07/11
- The Great War, in which he served in France, ends 11/18
- Brother Albert's wedding increases talk about his own future 04/23
- Criticism of his behaviour on South American tour 10/25
- On a visit to Canada with brother George, buys a ranch 09/26
- Is called home from Africa as his father lies gravely ill 11/28
- Father orders him to join the economy drive 11/31
- Severs contact with his close friend, Mrs Freda Dudley Ward 06/34
- Causes grave offence by presenting Mrs Simpson at court 11/34
- His blatant affair with Mrs Simpson is causing a scandal 12/34
- His father is dead, his mother kisses his hand in homage 01/36
- Upon the death of his father, is proclaimed King Edward VIII 01/36
- Neglects his duties as king, embarrasses the government 07/36
- Allows Mrs Simpson to act as hostess at an official dinner 07/36
- Cruises the Adriatic with Wallis; press barons smother facts 08/36
- Tells his family of his intention to marry Mrs Simpson 11/36
- Visiting Wales, he declares "something must be done" 11/36
- His remarks in Wales are being seen as political 11/36
- Refuses to speak to the Duke of York 12/36
- The country now knows of his love for a married woman 12/36
- Tells the Duke of York of his abdication 12/36
- Signs the Instrument of Abdication at Buckingham Palace 12/36
- Broadcasts to the nation, explaining why he is abdicating 12/36
- Pledges allegiance to King George VI 12/36
- Says goodbye to his family then slips away into exile 12/36
- Goes to Austria to await Mrs Simpson's divorce 12/36
- Marries the woman for whom he renounced his throne 06/37
- In Berlin with the Duchess, Hitler welcomes them warmly 10/37
- Receives a visit from Neville Chamberlain 11/38
- Causes embarrassment by a Nazi salute whilst visiting Hitler 1939
- Agitates for an "appropriate job" in Britain 1939

- Makes a broadcast seen as an attempt to undermine the king 05/39
- Offered a post at the Military Mission in Paris, he accepts 11/39
- Appointed Governor of the Bahamas 07/40
- Gets icy reception from Queen Mother at the king's funeral 02/52
- Queen Mother greets him at event commemorating Queen Mary 06/67
- Dies, three weeks after his niece, the queen, visits him 05/72

Windsor, Wallis, Duchess of
- Meets the Duchess of York at Fort Belvedere 01/33
- Perceived to be "queening it" over the prince's entourage 12/34
- Acts as hostess at an official Buckingham Palace dinner 07/36
- Files for divorce at Ipswich 10/36
- Has fled to France to escape the furore 12/36
- Marries the duke but is not granted the title Royal Highness 06/37
- A warm welcome for her and the duke from Hitler in Berlin 10/37
- Chamberlain visits the couple in Paris 11/38
- Dies in Paris 04/86

——————— X – Y – Z ———————

York, Elizabeth, Duchess of future queen
- See: Elizabeth, Queen, The Queen Mother

York, Prince Albert, Duke of future King George VI
- See: George VI, King

York, Prince Andrew, Duke of
- The second son born to Queen Elizabeth II 02/60
- Flies his naval helicopter in the Falkland conflict 06/82
- Marries Sarah Ferguson at Westminster Abbey 07/86
- His wife has a daughter, Princess Beatrice 08/88
- A second daughter, Princess Eugenie, is born 03/90
- Separates from his wife 1992
- Divorces the Duchess of York 04/96

York, Princess Beatrice of
- Born to the Duke and Duchess of York, 8 August 1988

York, Princess Eugenie of
- Born to the Duke and Duchess of York, 23 March 1990

York, Sarah, Duchess of
- Marries Prince Andrew at Westminster Abbey 07/86
- Gives birth to a daughter, Princess Beatrice 08/88
- She and her husband attract criticism over their lifestyle 08/89
- Gives birth to a second daughter, Princess Eugenie 03/90
- Separates from her husband 1992
- The queen refuses to help her pay off her debts 01/96
- Divorces Prince Andrew 04/96